Pages of
ENGLISH PROSE
1390–1930

Pages of ENGLISH PROSE 1390–1930

SELECTED BY
Sir Arthur Quiller-Couch

Oxford
AT THE CLARENDON PRESS
1930

OXFORD UNIVERSITY PRESS
AMEN HOUSE, E.C. 4
LONDON EDINBURGH GLASGOW
LEIPZIG NEW YORK TORONTO
MELBOURNE CAPETOWN BOMBAY
CALCUTTA MADRAS SHANGHAI
HUMPHREY MILFORD
PUBLISHER TO THE
UNIVERSITY

PRINTED IN GREAT BRITAIN

PREFACE

ALL but a few of the extracts in this little volume were selected by me at the request of the *Daily Mail's* Literary Editor, who wished to remind his readers of certain noble prose passages which every one means to read, some day, or else has read and forgotten. At the request of many correspondents and with his leave, they are here brought together in a handy form. He has also, and most kindly, allowed me to reprint the brief introductory notes which headed the various 'specimens'.

The history of our Country has ever abounded in occasions fit for lofty discussion at the time and afterwards for records worthily written; nor do these occasions grow fewer as time goes on or diminish in importance. Even in the hurry of this age men must pause at times to wonder at the inventions and discoveries they have lived to see, the crises of War and Politics in which they held their breath, the shocks through which they have passed through surprise to familiarity of custom, through peril to deliverance; and at the mysteries of birth, life, death, which are still the background of our stage. It is well, I think, that we should remind ourselves by examples, and let our children be taught in school to prize as a nation the language in which great writers have told of such things, and to maintain it level with our future. It has for a long while been fashionable to decry 'tall writing' in serious prose or even more damningly to dismiss it as a taken-for-granted fault. Strange to say, this almost axiomatic condemnation by any 'intellectual' weekly Review will run, within its covers, alongside the most extravagant language about a concert in Queen's Hall, or a new fashionable novel, or anything suggested to a new poet by something in a pond. On all these subjects the editor, in the second half of his paper and the third, fourth, or fifth reviews, just lets the superlative fly.

But in ordinary life I take it that this distrust or suspicion of 'the purple patch' has gone along with a gradual decline in the value of the noble art of rhetoric, of which I shall presently indicate some promise of revival.

For the present rhetoric is under the weather, save on political platforms—the humbug of which most decent Englishmen have learnt to despise, and the more to despise when they see former hopes chained to a body of corruption. But, apart from this, the mass, accumulation and press of business forbid all but infrequent outbreaks of rhetoric in Parliament. There was never quite enough time for a Burke in the British Senate. There is now no room. Even in the ordinary County Council, on which more and more business is being heaped, the quarterly agenda-paper with reports of committees will occupy some hundreds of pages—all to be disposed of at a sitting. What room for oratory here?

Then take sermons. Can we, in these days of Sunday golf and escape-from-business, even conceive of that appetite in our forefathers which drew them to throng and stand on their feet and listen rapturously for an hour and three-quarters to a sermon by Dean Donne in Old St. Paul's? Take the theatre. Shakespeare's audiences loved rhetoric so much that all listened expectant when, for example, Wolsey was left solus and

—he pausing a moment, the theatre hushed—began his farewell to all his greatness. Rhetoric was coming, with such elocution and gesture as the actor could compass, actor helping playwright to pay this due which custom prescribed. Nor did either confine their magnificence to the soliloquies. The playwright, playing up to an expensive stock-wardrobe of velvets and spangles—following also the 'rules' he read into Aristotle—packed his drama with kings and princes, lords and courtiers. Into their mouths he put such language as he conceived to befit persons of high degree; and the actor abetting gave these speeches their due sonorousness. Though the actual mask of 'old' Tragedy had gone, the buskin remained.

Thus there grew and persisted a fine tradition of oratory on our British stage—until 'realism' destroyed it. Conventional it may have been: unsuited to modern drama, whether to the woes of mechanics or to smart back-chat, it undoubtedly is; but at least it was articulate, it rendered the accent and music of Shakespeare audibly, and from the lips of Sir Johnston Forbes-Robertson or Dame Ellen Terry, *hodie deflenda*, it was a delight to hear. I recall a performance of *Romeo and Juliet* in which, barring the shaky yet distinct vocables of Ellen Terry as Nurse, not one articulate line reached the stalls during the three acts I had the fortitude to endure. All others in the cast, who should have been 'matched in mouth like bells', mumbled confused half-hearted noises. They were afraid of Shakespeare.

Rhetoric, in fine, persists among us but in that most conservative of all our institutions, the Law Courts, protected by wigs and protracted to a fine Athenian

PREFACE

length by fees. In our prose writing we funk it as our actors funk Shakespeare: and the 'purple patch' has become anathema.

But do we really prefer the dismal inheritance of Bentham and Grote and John Stuart Mill to our Burke, our Cobbett, our Ruskin, our Carlyle, with their fits of passion and extravagance? What is the matter with this Tyrian purple? True, it must be worn by a real man robed in his high argument and will not sit properly on the back of a dwarfish thief. As the most purple of English writers, Sir Thomas Browne, warns us—unconsciously staking his own reputation—'Seek not for Whales in the Euxine Sea, or expect great matters where they are not to be found. Seek not for profundity in shallowness . . .' The Athenian and the Roman after him alike, though in different fashion, prized rhetoric and taught it in their schools as a necessary part of a liberal education. Yet we know what frolic has Socrates made with the pretensions of charlatan instructors in that art; and, centuries later (say about A.D. 250), Longinus, who worshipped noble diction and has left us a priceless little tractate upon it, says soundly: 'Elsewhere I have written that "sublimity of speech is the echo of a noble soul. . . ." It is by all means necessary to point this out—that the truly eloquent must be free from base and ignoble or ill-bred thoughts. Great accents we expect to fall from the lips of those whose thoughts are dignified.' The late Earl of Oxford and Asquith exemplified this virtue for us in our day.

By temperament, however, Lord Oxford avoided as a rule the purple patch; and it is the purple patch I would defend here, as I tried to defend it some two or three years ago in my preface to a certain *Oxford Book of English Prose*. Literature, after all, is memorable speech: just that and no more (as I am always preaching at Cambridge to those who honour me as listeners), words worthy to be stored up in memory, writing, print, for our mental or spiritual improvement, language being the divinest of human gifts and apart from music and the pictorial arts the one medium, more plastic than either, of expressing his deepest thoughts and emotions. In this simple conception nice distinctions—definitions, for instance, of the 'proper' limits between poetry and prose—simply disappear. It suffices that something has been said which in itself or for its manner our fellows hold worthy of record, for their good. And in practice literature, even prose literature, will be found much more on the side of the purple patch than most people nowadays assume. Thucydides sewed these patches on to his narrative as a matter of course: he gave Pericles' famous oration, as hearers remembered it or as he dressed it up, as confidently as any historian of the American Civil War will include Lincoln's Gettysburg oration. Plato—as in his fable of the Gods in Procession—habitually uses high poetical prose and parable when his philosophy shades off into the deeper mysteries. Cicero draped himself in such purple: so, in the line of our own prose in their turn and on given occasion, did Donne, Milton, Browne, Berkeley, Gibbon, Johnson, De Quincey, Hazlitt, Macaulay—to come no nearer. Nay, if we go right back (I have contended), it is arguable that Prose was 'born in the purple': that nine-tenths of the speech-making in the *Iliad* itself, for example, is rhetoric strung into hexameters.

PREFACE

For those who have not the leisure to taste the fine enjoyment of following (say) a Milton or a Burke as their great arguments (and their arguments are habitually great), starting from pedestrian levels, wind up in ample circuits, then, narrowing up with closer spiral, shoot suddenly aloft in passion, or as when St. Paul, after a long, sinuous, and (to tell the truth) somewhat sophisticated argument on Death and Resurrection, astounds us with that tremendous outburst beginning 'Behold, I show you a mystery', I believe that to acquaint themselves with a number of these high passages —oftener taken for granted than studied—the references to which I append, will do some good, since that spirit attracts spirit is no less certain than that matter attracts matter.

Q.

CONTENTS

Sir Thomas Malory, fl. 1470
THE LAST MEETING OF LAUNCELOT AND GUENEVER (*Le Morte Arthur*) . . . 1
SIR ECTOR'S DIRGE OVER SIR LAUNCELOT (*Le Morte Arthur*) 3

Richard Hakluyt, 1552?–1616
THE FIRST LANDING IN VIRGINIA (*Principall Navigations, Voiages, and Discoveries of the English Nation*) 5

Sir Walter Raleigh, 1552–1618
DEATH (*A History of the World*) 9

Sir Philip Sidney, 1554–1586
'WITH A TALE HE COMETH' (*An Apologie for Poetrie*) 11

Richard Hooker, 1554–1600
LAWS OF NATURE (*The Laws of Ecclesiastical Polity*) 12

Sir Ranulphe Crewe, 1558–1646
ON THE EARLDOM OF OXFORD (*Law Reports*) 14

Francis Bacon, 1561–1626
THE SERVICE OF THE MUSES (*Essex's Device*) 16
OF STUDIES (*Essays*) 17

William Shakespeare, 1564–1616
HAMLET ON MAN (*Hamlet, Act II, Scene 2*) . 18

John Donne, 1573–1631
DEATH THE LEVELLER (*LXXX Sermons*) . 19

CONTENTS

William Drummond of Hawthornden, 1585–1649
ON DYING YOUNG (*The Cypresse Grove*) . . 20

Izaak Walton, 1593–1683
A MILKMAID'S SONG (*The Compleat Angler*) . 21

John Earle, 1601–1665
A CHILD (*Microcosmographie*) 23

Sir Thomas Browne, 1605–1682
PULVIS ET UMBRA SUMUS (*Urn Burial*) . 25
THE HEROICK MIND (*Christian Morals*) . . 26

Thomas Fuller, 1608–1661
WYCLIFFE'S ASHES (*Church History of England*) . 27

John Milton, 1608–1674
THE TYRANNY OF LICENSING (*Areopagitica*) 28

Edward Hyde, 1609–1674
CHARACTER OF LORD FALKLAND (*A History of the Rebellion*) 29

Old Testament, 1611
I. 'THINE EYES SHALL SEE THE KING' (Isaiah xxxiii. 17–24) 31
II. 'ARISE, SHINE' (Isaiah lx. 1–3, 19–20) . 32
III. 'REMEMBER NOW THY CREATOR' (Ecclesiastes xii) 32
IV. 'THE VOICE OF MY BELOVED' (Song of Solomon ii. 8–17; v. 2–8) 34

New Testament, 1611
ST. PAUL ON DEATH (1 Corinthians xv. 51–end) 35

Apocrypha
'GOD'S PURPOSE IS ETERNAL' (2 Esdras vi. 1–6) 36

CONTENTS

The English Liturgy
COLLECTS FROM THE FIRST PRAYER BOOK OF EDWARD VI, 1549, i, ii, and iii. . 37

John Holland, fl. 1638
A DISCOURSE OF THE NAVY (*John Holland: First Discourse of the Navy*) 38

Jeremy Taylor, 1613–1667
AGAINST BITTERNESS OF ZEAL (*Sermons*) . 40

John Bunyan, 1628–1688
THE VALLEY OF HUMILIATION . . 42
MR. VALIANT-FOR-TRUTH CROSSES THE RIVER (*Pilgrim's Progress*) 43

John Dryden, 1631–1700
3 JUNE, 1665 (*Essay of Dramatic Poesy*) . . 44

The Marquess of Halifax, 1633–1695
LOOK TO YOUR MOAT (*A Rough Draft of a New Model at Sea*) 46

Samuel Pepys, 1633–1703
A JAUNT INTO THE COUNTRY (*Diary*, 14 June 1667) 48

Thomas Traherne, 1636–1674
THE HEIR OF ALL THINGS (*Centuries of Meditations*) 52

Daniel Defoe, c. 1659–1731
THE FOOT-PRINT (*Robinson Crusoe*) . . 53

Jonathan Swift, 1667–1745
A STANDARD FOR ENGLISH (*Letter Dedicatory to the Earl of Oxford*) 55
GULLIVER CAPTURES THE FLEET OF BLEFUSCU (*A Voyage to Lilliput*) 56

CONTENTS

Joseph Addison, 1672–1719
WESTMINSTER ABBEY (*The Spectator*) . . 59

Henry Fielding, 1707–1754
LONDON RIVER (*Journal of a Voyage to Lisbon*) . 60

Samuel Johnson, 1709–1784
LETTER TO LORD CHESTERFIELD . 62
ON HIS ENGLISH DICTIONARY . . 64

Laurence Sterne, 1713–1768
THE DEATH OF LE FEVER (*Tristram Shandy*) . 66

Oliver Goldsmith, 1728–1774
A PARTY AT VAUXHALL (*Citizen of the World*) 67

Edmund Burke, 1729–1797
MARIE ANTOINETTE (*Reflections on the Revolution in France*) 71

Edward Gibbon, 1734–1794
GIBBON ON HIS LIFE WORK (*Memoirs of My Life and Writings*) 73

William Wordsworth, 1770–1850
THE POET (Preface to *Lyrical Ballads*) . . 74

Sir Walter Scott, 1771–1832
THE LAIRD EVICTS THE GYPSIES (*Guy Mannering*) 76
THE BANNER OF ENGLAND (*The Talisman*) 80

Charles Lamb, 1775–1834
DREAM CHILDREN (*Essays of Elia*) . . 82

Walter Savage Landor, 1775–1864
AESOP AND RHODOPE (*Imaginary Conversations*) 83

CONTENTS

William Hazlitt, 1778–1830
JOHN CAVANAGH (*Table-Talk*) . . . 85

Thomas De Quincey, 1785–1859
OUR LADIES OF SORROW (*Suspira de Profundis*) 89

Sir William Napier, 1785–1860
ALBUERA (*History of the Peninsular War*) . . 92

Thomas Carlyle, 1795–1881
JOCELIN OF BRAKELOND (*Past and Present*) . 94

Thomas Babington Macaulay, 1800–1859
THE SIEGE OF LONDONDERRY (*History of England from the Accession of James I*) . . . 96

John Henry Newman, 1801–1890
DEFINITION OF A GENTLEMAN (*The Idea of a University*) 97

Abraham Lincoln, 1809–1865
GETTYSBURG (*Dedicatory Address at Gettysburg Cemetery, Nov. 19, 1863*) 99

Edward FitzGerald, 1809–1883
THE BOAT RACE (*Euphranor*) 101

William Makepeace Thackeray, 1811–1863
PULVIS ET UMBRA (*Esmond*) 102

John Bright, 1811–1889
THE ANGEL OF DEATH (*Speech in the House of Commons on the Crimean War, Feb. 23, 1855*) . . 104

Charles Dickens, 1812–1870
DAVID'S LIBRARY (*David Copperfield*) . . 106
MRS. GAMP ON STEAM-ENGINES (*Martin Chuzzlewit*) 107

John Lothrop Motley, 1814–1877
WILLIAM OF ORANGE (*The Dutch Republic*) . 112

CONTENTS

James Anthony Froude, 1818–1894
THE TAKING OF THE *CACAFUEGO* (*English Seamen in the Sixteenth Century*) 114

George Eliot, 1819–1880
MAGGIE AND THE DOLL (*The Mill on the Floss*) 117

Walt Whitman, 1819–1892
STARLIGHT, AND CARLYLE DYING (*Specimen Days in America*) 119

John Ruskin, 1819–1900
A CATHEDRAL CLOSE (*The Stones of Venice*) . 121

Matthew Arnold, 1822–1888
CHARM OF OXFORD 124

George Meredith, 1828–1909
DAWN IN THE MOUNTAINS (*The Amazing Marriage*) 125

Algernon Charles Swinburne, 1837–1909
BYRON (Introduction to a *Selection from the Works of Lord Byron*) 128

Walter Pater, 1839–1894
MONA LISA (*The Renaissance*) . . . 129

Thomas Hardy, 1840–1928
MIDNIGHT ON ST. THOMAS'S EVE (*Far From the Madding Crowd*) 130

Robert Louis Stevenson, 1850–1894
THE ENGLISH ADMIRALS (*Virginibus Puerisque*) 132

Lytton Strachey, 1880–
THE PASSING OF QUEEN VICTORIA (*Queen Victoria*) 133

Sir Thomas Malory

SIR THOMAS MALORY (d. 1471) belonged to an old Warwickshire family, and served in the retinue of the Earl of Warwick (afterwards the Kingmaker) in France. He lived, that is to say, at the close of the period which we call the Middle Ages. He spent some time in prison about 1468, perhaps on account of the part he took in the Wars of the Roses, and it was then that he wrote large parts, if not all, of the *Morte Arthur*, the history of King Arthur and his knights, and of the achieving of the Sangreal. This is, at the end of the Middle Ages, a kind of romance or novel of and about the Middle Ages. It is derived from the great medieval Arthurian legends, and it was written for the same reason that Caxton later gave for printing it: 'to the entente that noble men take the good and honest actes in their remembrance, and folowe the same.' The two extracts given below are from the close, after the last battle, when the chivalry of the Table has been destroyed and the King slain. Sir Lancelot takes final leave of the Queen, and a year afterwards, when he has died, a hermit, Sir Ector laments over his body.

¶ THE LAST MEETING OF LAUNCELOT AND GUENEVER

From LE MORTE ARTHUR

SO it was no bote[1] to stryve, but he departed and rode westerly, & there he sought a vij or viij dayes, & atte last he cam to a nonnerye, & than was quene Guenever ware of sir Launcelot as he walked in the cloystre. And whan she sawe hym there she swouned thryse, that al the ladyes & Ientyl wymmen had werke ynough to holde the quene up. So whan she myght speke she callyd ladyes & Ientyl wymmen to hir & sayd, Ye mervayl, fayr ladyes, why I make this fare.[2] Truly,

---

[1] *bote*] good   [2] *fare*] stir

she said, it is for the syght of yonder knyght that yender standeth. Wherfore, I praye you al, calle hym to me. Whan syr Launcelot was brought to hyr, than she sayd to al the ladyes, Thorowe this man & me hath al this warre be wrought, & the deth of the moost noblest knyghtes of the world. For thorugh our love that we have loved togyder is my moost noble lord slayn. Therfor, syr Launcelot, wyt thou wel I am sette in suche a plyte to gete my soule hele. & yet I truste thorugh Goddes grace that after my deth to have a syght of the blessyd face of Cryst, and at domes day to sytte on his ryght syde, for as synful as ever I was are sayntes in heven. Therfore, syr Launcelot, I requyre the & beseche the hertelye, for al the love that ever was betwyxte us, that thou never see me more in the vysage, & I comande the on goddes behalfe that thou forsake my companye, & to thy kyngdom thou torne[1] ageyn & kepe wel thy royame from warre & wrake. For as wel as I have loved the, myn hert wyl not serve me to see the, for thorugh the & me is the flour of kynges & knyghtes destroyed. Therfor, sir Launcelot, goo to thy royame, & there take the a wyf, & lyve with hir with Ioye & blysse. & I praye the hertelye praye for me to our Lord, that I may amende my myslyvyng. Now, swete madam, sayd syr Launcelot, wold ye that I shold torne ageyn unto my cuntreye & there to wedde a lady? Nay, Madam, wyt you wel that shal I never do, for I shal never be soo fals to you of that I have promysed, but the same deystenye that ye have taken you to I wyl take me unto, for to plese Iesu, & ever for you I cast me specially to praye. Yf thou wylt do so, sayd the quene, holde thy promyse. But I may never byleve but that

[1] *torne*] turn

thou wylt torne to the world ageyn. Wel, madam, sayd he, ye say as pleseth you, yet wyst you me never fals of my promesse, & God defende but I shold forsake the world as ye have do. For in the quest of the Sank Greal I had forsaken the vanytees of the world had not your lord ben. And yf I had done so at that tyme wyth my herte, wylle and thought, I had passed al the knyghtes that were in the Sanke Greal, excepte syr Galahad my sone. And therfore, lady, sythen ye have taken you to perfeccion, I must nedys take me to perfection of ryght. For I take recorde of God, in you I have had myn erthly Ioye. And yf I had founden you now so dysposed I had caste me to have had you in to myn owne royame. But sythen I fynde you thus desposed I ensure you faythfully I wyl ever take me to penaunce, & praye whyle my lyf lasteth, yf that I may fynde ony heremyte other[1] graye or whyte that wyl receyve me. Wherfore, madame, I praye you kysse me, & never nomore. Nay, sayd the quene, that shal I never do, but absteyne you from suche werkes; & they departed.[2]

¶ SIR ECTOR'S DIRGE OVER LAUNCELOT

AND soo the bysshop & they al togydere wente wyth the body of syr Launcelot dayly, tyl they came to Ioyous garde. And ever they had an C torches bernnyng aboute hym; & so within xv dayes they came to Ioyous garde. And there they layed his corps in the body of the quere, & sange & redde many saulters & prayers over hym and aboute hym, & ever his vysage was layed open & naked that al folkes myght beholde hym. For suche was the custom in tho dayes, that al men of

---

[1] *other*] either   [2] *departed*] separated

worshyp shold so lye wyth open vysage tyl that they were buryed. And ryght thus as they were at theyr servyce there came syr Ector de Maris, that had vij yere sought al Englond, Scotland & Walys, sekyng his brother syr Launcelot. And whan syr Ector herde suche noyse & lyghte in the quyre of Ioyous garde he alyght, & put his hors from hym, & came in to the quyre, & there he sawe men synge & wepe. And al they knewe syr Ector, but he knewe not them. Than wente syr Bors unto syr Ector, & tolde hym how there laye his brother syr Launcelot dede. And than Syr Ector threwe hys shelde, swerde & helme from hym; and whan he behelde syr Launcelottes vysage he fyl doun in a swoun, & whan he waked it were harde ony tonge to telle the doleful complayntes that he made for his brother. A, Launcelot, he sayd, thou were hede of al crysten knyghtes; & now I dare say, sayd syr Ector, thou sir Launcelot, there thou lyest, that thou were never matched of erthely knyghtes hande; & thou were the curtest[1] knyght that ever bare shelde; & thou were the truest frende to thy lover that ever bestrade hors; & thou were the trewest lover of a synful man that ever loved woman; & thou were the kyndest man that ever strake wyth werde; & thou were the godelyest persone that ever cam emonge prees[2] of knyghtes; & thou was the mekest man & the Ientyllest that ever ete in halle emonge ladyes; & thou were the sternest knyght to thy mortal foo that ever put spere in the breste. Than there was wepyng & dolour out of mesure. Thus they kepte syr Launcelots corps on lofte[3] xv dayes, & than they buryed it with grete devocyon.

[1] *curtest*] most courteous   [2] *prees*] crowd
[3] *on lofte*] above ground

Richard Hakluyt

RICHARD HAKLUYT (1552?–1616), Archdeacon of Westminster and geographer. He had while still at Oxford read 'whatever printed or written discoveries and voyages I found extant, either in Greek, Latin, Italian, Spanish, Portugal, French, or English languages'. In 1589 he produced the *Principall Navigations, Voiages, and Discoveries of the English Nation*—one volume dedicated to Sir Francis Walsingham; it was reissued, much enlarged, in three volumes, in 1598–1600. He was excited to this by 'not seeing any man to have care to recommend to the world the industrious labours and painful travels of our countrymen'. His explorations of this kind were as valuable to our literature as those of his heroes had been to our statecraft, commerce, and dominion.

¶ THE FIRST LANDING IN VIRGINIA

From PRINCIPALL NAVIGATIONS, VOIAGES, AND DISCOVERIES OF THE ENGLISH NATION

The First Voyage made to the coasts of America, with two barks, wherein were Captains Master Philip Amadas, and Master Arthur Barlow, who discovered part of the country now called Virginia, anno 1584.

THE second of July we found shoal water, which smelt so sweetly, and was so strong a smell, as if we had been in the midst of some delicate garden, abounding with all kinds of odoriferous flowers; by which we were assured that the land could not be far distant. And keeping good watch and bearing but slack sail, the fourth of the same month we arrived upon the coast, which we supposed to be a continent and firm land, and we sailed along the same 120 English miles before we could find any entrance, or river issuing into the Sea. The first that appeared unto us we entered, though not without some difficulty, and cast anchor about three arquebus-shot within the haven's mouth, on the left hand of the same; and after thanks given to God for our safe arrival thither, we manned our boats, and went to view the land next adjoining, and to take possession of the same in the right of the Queen's most excellent Majesty, as rightful Queen and Princess of the same, and after delivered the same over to your use, according to her Majesty's grant and letters patents, under her Highness's great Seal. Which being performed, according to the ceremonies used in such enterprises, we viewed the land about us, being, whereas we first landed, very sandy and low towards the water side, but so full of grapes as the very beating and surge of the sea overflowed them. Of which we found such plenty, as well there as in all places else, both on the sand and on the green soil on the hills, as in the plains, as well on every little shrub, as also climbing towards the tops of high Cedars, that I think in all the world the like abundance is not to be found: and myself having seen those parts of Europe that most abound, find such difference as were incredible to be written.

We passed from the sea side towards the tops of those hills next adjoining, being but of mean height; and from thence we beheld the Sea on both sides, to the North and to the South, finding no end any of both ways. This land lay stretching itself to the West, which after we found to be but an Island of twenty leagues long, and not above six miles broad. Under the bank or hill whereon we stood, we beheld the valleys replenished with goodly Cedar trees, and having discharged our arquebus-shot, such a flock of Cranes (the most part white) arose under us, with such a cry redoubled by many Echoes, as if an army of men had shouted all together.

This Island had many goodly woods, and full of Deer, Coneys, Hares, and Fowl, even in the midst of Summer, in incredible abundance. The woods are not such as you find in *Bohemia*, *Moscovia*, or *Hyrcania*, barren and fruitless, but the highest and reddest cedars of the world, far bettering the Cedars of the *Azores*, of the *Indias*, or of *Libanus*; Pines, Cypress, Sassafras, the Lentisk, or the tree that beareth the Mastic; the tree that beareth the rind of black Cinnamon, of which Master *Winter* brought from the Straits of *Magellan*; and many other of excellent smell and quality. We remained by the side of this Island two whole days before we saw any people of the Country. The third day we espied one small boat rowing towards us, having in it three persons. This boat came to the land's side, four arquebus-shot from our ships; and there two of the people remaining, the third came along the shore side towards us, and we being then all within board, he walked up and down upon the point of the land next unto us. Then the Master and the Pilot of the Admiral, *Simon Ferdinando*, and the Captain, *Philip Amadas*, myself, and others, rowed to the land; whose coming this fellow attended, never making any show of fear or doubt. And after he had spoken of many things not understood by us, we brought him, with his own good liking, aboard the ships, and gave him a shirt, a hat, and some other things, and made him taste of our wine and our meat, which he liked very well; and, after having viewed both barks, he departed, and went to his own boat again, which he had left in a little Cove or Creek adjoining. As soon as he was two bow-shot into the water he fell to fishing, and in less than half an hour he had laden his boat as deep as it could swim, with which he came again to the point of the land, and there he divided his fish into two parts, pointing one part to the ship and the other to the pinnace. Which, after he had as much as he might requited the former benefits received, departed out of our sight.

The next day there came unto us divers boats, and in one of them the King's brother, accompanied with forty or fifty men, very handsome and goodly people, and in their behaviour as mannerly and civil as any of Europe. His name was *Granganimeo*, and the king is called *Wingina*; the country, *Wingandacoa*, (and now by her Majesty *Virginia*). The manner of his coming was in this sort: he left his boats altogether as the first man did, a little from the ships by the shore, and came along to the place over against the ships, followed with forty men. When he came to the place, his servants spread a long mat upon the ground, on which he sat down, and at the other end of the mat four others of his company did the like; the rest of his men stood round about him somewhat afar off. When we came to the shore to him, with our weapons, he never moved from his place, nor any of the other four, nor never mistrusted any harm to be offered from us; but, sitting still, he beckoned us to come and sit by him, which we performed; and being set, he makes all signs of joy and welcome, striking on his head and his breast and afterwards on ours, to show we were all one, smiling and making show the best he could of all love and familiarity. After he had made a long speech unto us we presented him with divers things, which he received very joyfully and thankfully. None of the company durst to speak one word all the time; only the four which were at the other end spake one in the other's ear very softly.

Sir Walter Raleigh

SIR WALTER RALEIGH (1552-1618) is known much more widely as a favourite of Queen Elizabeth than as an author. But some of his poems are still to be read in anthologies, and the extract below is a famous 'purple patch' of English prose. It comes from his *History of the World*, which he wrote when, after a career of foreign adventure and discovery, and of varying Court favour, he was sent to the Tower in 1603 under James I. He remained there till 1616, when he was allowed to undertake an expedition to the Orinoco. He was executed in 1618.

¶ DEATH

From A HISTORY OF THE WORLD

FOR the rest, if we seek a reason of the succession and continuance of this boundless ambition in mortal men, we may add to that which hath been already said; That the Kings and Princes of the world have always laid before them the actions, but not the ends, of those great Ones which preceded them. They are always transported with the glory of the one, but they never mind the misery of the other till they find the experience in themselves. They neglect the advice of God while they enjoy life, or hope it; but they follow the counsel of Death upon his first approach.

It is he that puts into man all the wisdom of the world without speaking a word; which God with all the words of his Law promises, or threats, doth not infuse. Death, which hateth and destroyeth man, is believed; God, which hath made him and loves him, is always deferred. I have considered (saith Solomon) all the works that are under the Sun, and behold, all is vanity and vexation of spirit: but who believes it till Death tells it us?

It was Death which, opening the conscience of Charles the Fifth, made him enjoin his son Philip to restore Navarre; and King Francis the First of France to command that justice should be done upon the Murderers of the Protestants in Merindol and Cabrieres, which till then he neglected.

It is therefore Death alone that can suddenly make man to know himself. He tells the proud and insolent that they are but Abjects, and humbles them at the instant; makes them cry, complain, and repent, yea, even to hate their forepassed happiness.

He takes the account of the rich and proves him a beggar; a naked beggar which hath interest in nothing but in the gravel that fills his mouth. He holds a Glass before the eyes of the most beautiful, and makes them see therein their deformity and rottenness; and they acknowledge it.

O eloquent, just, and mighty Death! whom none could advise, thou hast persuaded; what none hath dared thou hast done; and whom all the world hath flattered, thou only hast cast out of the world and despised: thou hast drawn together all the farstretched greatness, all the pride, cruelty, and ambition of man, and covered it all over with these two narrow words, *Hic jacet.*

Sir Philip Sidney

SIR PHILIP SIDNEY (1554–86) was an ambassador at 23 and an M.P. for Kent at 27. He was Governor of Flushing at 31. His *Apologie for Poetrie* is the first important contribution to English literary criticism; and he wrote some beautiful sonnets which gave the sonnet sequence its first vogue in England.

¶ 'WITH A TALE HE COMETH'

From AN APOLOGIE FOR POETRIE

NOW therein of all Sciences (I speak still of humane, and according to the humane conceits) is our Poet the Monarch. For he doth not only show the way, but giveth so sweet a prospect into the way, as will entice any man to enter into it.

Nay, he doth, as if your journey should lie through a fair Vineyard, at the first give you a cluster of Grapes, that, full of that taste, you may long to passe further.

He beginneth not with obscure definitions, which must blur the margent with interpretations, and load the memory with doubtfulness; but he cometh to you with words set in delightful proportion, either accompanied with, or prepared for, the well enchanting skill of Musick; and with a tale forsooth he cometh unto you: with a tale which holdeth children from play, and old men from the chimney corner. And, pretending no more, doth intend the winning of the mind from wickedness to virtue: even as the child is often brought to take most wholesome things by hiding them in such other as have a pleasant taste: which, if one should begin to tell them the nature of Aloes or Rhubarb they shoud receive, would sooner take their Physick at their ears than at their mouth.

So is it in men (most of which are childish in the best things, till they be cradled in their graves); glad they will be to hear the tales of Hercules, Achilles, Cyrus, and Aeneas; and hearing them, must needs hear the right description of wisdom, valour, and justice; which, if they had been barely, that is to say, Philosophically set out, they would swear they be brought to school again.

Richard Hooker

COMPARATIVELY few English theologians are read after the period they wrote for has passed away, but Richard Hooker (1554–1600) has become a classic in literature as well as theology. He was for some time (1585–91) Master of the Temple, afterwards Rector of Boscombe, Wiltshire, and Bishopsbourne, Kent. His great work, the *Laws of Ecclesiastical Polity*, was a philosophic examination of the basis of Church government, and a defence of the Church of England against rival claims. The epithet 'judicious' often applied to him is descriptive at once of his personal quiet patience and industry; of his equable and careful thought; and of his subdued and stately prose. This has been called 'the first monument of splendid literary prose that we possess'. But its splendour is subordinate to its business of intellect.

¶ LAWS OF NATURE

From THE LAWS OF ECCLESIASTICAL POLITY

NOW if nature should intermit her course, and leave altogether though it were but for a while the observation of her own laws; if those principal and mother elements of the world, whereof all things in this lower world are made, should lose the qualities which now they have; if the frame of that heavenly arch erected over our heads should loosen and dissolve itself; if celestial spheres should forget their wonted motions, and by irregular volubility turn themselves any way as it might happen; if the prince of the lights of heaven, which now as a giant doth run his unwearied course, should as it were through a languishing faintness begin to stand and to rest himself; if the moon should wander from her beaten way, the times and seasons of the year blend themselves by disordered and confused mixture, the winds breathe out their last gasp, the clouds yield no rain, the earth be defeated of heavenly influence, the fruits of the earth pine away as children at the withered breasts of their mother no longer able to yield them relief: what would become of man himself, whom these things now do all serve? See we not plainly that obedience of creatures unto the law of nature is the stay of the whole world?

Sir Ranulphe Crewe

SIR RANULPHE CREWE (1558–1646), after a distinguished career as serjeant-at-law, became Lord Chief Justice in 1625, but was removed in November 1626 for refusing to subscribe a document affirming the legality of forced loans. The speech which follows is said to be one of the few passages of fine prose to be found in the *Law Reports*, and was delivered during his occupation of the Chief Justiceship. The direct male line of the earls of Oxford had come to an end and the succession was contested. Crewe's own family is said to have been an ancient one, and it is this consciousness of antiquity which informs his speech on the illustrious line of the De Veres.

¶ ON THE EARLDOM OF OXFORD

THE RESOLUTION delivered by CREW, *chief justice in parliament, concerning the earldom of Oxford;* WALTER, *chief baron;* DODRIDGE *and* YELVERTON, *justices; and* TREVOR, *baron, advising with him together therein.*

MY LORDS,

THIS great and weighty cause, incomparable to any other that hath happened in any time, requires great deliberation, and solid and mature judgment to determine it; and therefore I wish all the judges of England had heard it, (being a case fit for all) to the end we all together might have given our humble advice to your lordships herein.

Here is represented unto your lordships *certamen honoris*, and as I may well say, *illustris honoris*, illustrious honour.

I heard a great peer of this realm and a learned, say, when he lived, there was no King in Christendom had such a subject as Oxford.

He came in with the conqueror earl of Gwynes, shortly after the conquest made great chamberlain of England, above five hundred years ago, by HENRY I, the Conqueror's son, brother to RUFUS; by MAWD, the Empress, earl of Oxford, confirmed and approved by HENRY FITZ EMPRESS, HENRY II, *Alberico comiti*, so earl before.

This great honour, this high and noble dignity, hath continued ever since in the remarkable sirname of DE VERE, by so many ages, descents and generations, as no other kingdom can produce such a peer in one and the self same name and title.

I find in all this length of time but two attainders of this noble family, and those in stormy and tempestuous times, when the government was unsettled, and the kingdom in competition.

I have laboured to make a covenant with myself, that affection may not press upon judgment; for I suppose there is no man, that hath any apprehension of gentry or nobleness, but his affection stands to the continuance of so noble a name and house, and would take hold of a twig or twine-thread to uphold it: and yet time hath his revolution, there must be a period and an end of all temporal things, *finis rerum*, an end of names and dignities, and whatsoever is terrene; and why not of DE VERE?

For where is BOHUN? where's MOWBRAY? where's MORTIMER? nay, which is more, and most of all, where is PLANTAGENET? They are intombed in the urns and sepulchres of mortality.

And yet let the name and dignity of DE VERE stand so long as it pleaseth God.

This case stands upon many parts.

Subtile disputants may perturb the best judgments; there have been many thick and dark fogs and mists raised in the face of this cause.

But *magna est veritas et prevalet*, truth lets in the sun to scatter and disperse them.

Francis Bacon

SIR FRANCIS BACON (1561–1626), Lord Verulam and Viscount St. Albans, was one of the many English statesmen who have also been great men of letters. He served King James I as Attorney-General and Lord Chancellor, and was the chief juristic defender of the Stewart theory of monarchy. He was a profound essayist, but his chief title to fame is that his Novum Organum gave a new basis to philosophy after the repudiation of the scholastic systems.

¶ THE SERVICE OF THE MUSES
From ESSEX'S DEVICE

LET thy master, Squire, offer his service to the Muses. It is long since they received any into their court. They give alms continually at their gate, that many come to live upon; but few have they ever admitted into their palace. There shall he find secrets not dangerous to know, sides and parties not factious to hold, precepts and commandments not penal to disobey. The gardens of love wherein he now playeth himself are fresh to-day and fading tomorrow, as the sun comforts them or is turned from them. But the gardens of the Muses keep the privilege of the golden age; they ever flourish and are in league with time. The monuments of wit survive the monuments of power; the verses of a poet endure without a syllable lost, while states and empires pass many periods. Let him not think he shall descend, for he is now upon a hill as a ship is mounted upon the ridge of a wave; but that hill of the Muses is above tempests, always clear and calm; a hill of the goodliest discovery that man can have, being a prospect upon all the errors and wanderings of the present and former times. Yea, in some cliff it leadeth the eye beyond the horizon of time, and giveth no obscure divinations of times to come. So that if he will indeed lead *vitam vitalem*, a life that unites safety and dignity, pleasure and merit; if he will win admiration without envy; if he will be in the feast and not in the throng, in the light and not in the heat; let him embrace the life of study and contemplation.

¶ OF STUDIES
From ESSAYS

READ not to contradict and confute, nor to believe and take for granted, nor to find talk and discourse, but to weigh and consider. Some *Books* are to be tasted, others to be swallowed, and some few to be chewed and digested; That is, some *Books* are to be read only in parts; others to be read but not curiously, and some few to be read wholly, and with diligence and attention. Some *Books* also may be read by deputy, and extracts made of them by others; but that would be only in the less important arguments and the meaner sort of *Books*; else distilled books are like common distilled waters, flashy things. Reading maketh a full man; Conference a ready man; and Writing an exact man; and therefore, if a man write little he had need have a great memory; if he confer little he had need have a present wit; and if he read little he had need have much cunning, to seem to know that he doth not. *Histories* make men wise; *Poets*, witty; the *Mathematicks*, subtile; *Natural Philosophy*, deep; *Moral*, grave; *Logick and Rhetorick*, able to contend: *Abeunt studia in mores.*

William Shakespeare

THIS purple patch is taken from the works of a man whose powers as a dramatist and poet are so transcendent that his prose is often forgotten. Shakespeare unfortunately left little prose. The fragments to be found scattered through his plays show, however, that had he chosen he could have been one of the greatest masters in this as in other veins. In its richness, wealth of imagery, music and power his prose is among the finest of an age that did this sort of thing superlatively well. The following is typical.

¶ HAMLET ON MAN
From HAMLET, *Act II, Scene II*

I HAVE of late—but wherefore I know not—lost all my mirth, forgone all custom of exercise; and indeed it goes so heavily with my disposition that this goodly frame, the Earth, seems to me a sterile Promontory; this most excellent Canopy, the Air, look you, this brave o'erhanging Firmament, this Majestical Roof fretted with golden fire, why, it appears no other thing to me than a foul and pestilent congregation of vapours. What a piece of work is a man! How Noble in Reason! how infinite in faculty! in form and moving, how express and admirable! in Action how like an Angel! in apprehension how like a God! the beauty of the world! the Paragon of Animals! And yet, to me, what is this Quintessence of Dust? Man delights not me; no, nor Woman neither, though, by your smiling, you seem to say so.

John Donne

JOHN DONNE (1573–1631), the son of a Catholic family, entered the Church of England and, in middle age, took Orders. He became chaplain to James I and a notable preacher, besides being the author of several volumes of amatory, satirical, devotional and philosophical verse. He was the founder of what Dryden called the metaphysical school of poetry. His sermons exercised, at a critical time, a profound influence on the development of English prose style.

¶ DEATH THE LEVELLER
From LXXX SERMONS: SERMON XV

IT comes equally to us all, and makes us all equal when it comes. The ashes of an Oak in the Chimney are no Epitaph of that Oak to tell me how high or how large that was; it tells me not what flocks it sheltered while it stood, nor what men it hurt when it fell. The dust of great persons' graves is speechless too, it says nothing, it distinguishes nothing; as soon the dust of a wretch whom thou wouldest not, as of a Prince thou couldest not look upon, will trouble thine eyes, if the wind blow it thither; and when a whirlwind hath blown the dust of the Churchyard into the Church, and the man sweeps out the dust of the Church into the Churchyard, who will undertake to sift those dusts again, and to pronounce, This is the Patrician, this is the noble flower, and this the yeomanly, this the Plebeian bran. So is the death of Jesabel (Jesabel was a Queen) expressed; They shall not say, this is Jesabel; not only not wonder that it is, nor pity that it should be, but they shall not say, they shall not know, This is Jesabel.

William Drummond

WILLIAM DRUMMOND (1585–1649) of Hawthornden, near Edinburgh, is generally remembered rather by the fact that Ben Jonson visited him in 1618 than by his own work, though a few of his poems appear in anthologies. *The Cypresse-Grove*, published in 1623, is a philosophic meditation on death, and is, as it were, an essay in that style which Sir Thomas Browne was afterwards to perfect. Drummond has neither the intellectual vastness of Browne's phrases nor the sonority of his diction. But he has his own mortal solemnity, and his prose, being simpler, is perhaps more poignant than his later contemporary's.

¶ OF DYING YOUNG
From THE CYPRESSE GROVE

BUT that, perhaps, which anguisheth thee most, is to have this glorious Pageant of the World removed from thee, in the Spring and most delicious Season of thy Life; for though to die be usual, to die young may appear extraordinary. If the present Fruition of these Things be unprofitable and vain, What can a long Continuance of them be? If God had made Life happier, he had also made it longer. Stranger and new Halcyon, why would thou longer nestle amidst these unconstant and stormy Waves? Hast thou not already suffered enough of this World, but thou must yet endure more? To live long, is it not to be long troubled? But number thy Years, which are now ✱✱✱ and thou shalt find, that whereas Ten have outlived thee, Thousands have not attained this Age. One Year is sufficient to behold all the Magnificence of Nature, nay, even One Day and Night; for more is but the same brought again. This Sun, that Moon, these Stars, the varying Dance of the Spring, Summer, Autumn, Winter, is that very same which the Golden Age did see. They which have the longest Time lent them to live in, have almost no Part of it at all, measuring it either by the Space of Time which is past, when they were not, or by that which is to come. Why shouldst thou then care, whether thy Days be many or few, which, when prolonged to the uttermost, prove, paralleled with Eternity, as a Tear is to the Ocean? To die young, is to do that soon, and in some fewer Days, which once thou must do; it is but the giving over of a Game, that after never so many Hazards, must be lost.

Izaak Walton

IZAAK WALTON (1593–1683), by trade an ironmonger and by recreation a fisherman, was a man of one book, but that a masterpiece. *The Compleat Angler* is not only a complete guide to the psychology of fish and the methods of their capture, but a revelation of its author's personality. His gentle humour and mellow kindliness are in refreshing contrast to the stormy time in which he lived.

¶ A MILKMAID'S SONG

From THE COMPLEAT ANGLER

BUT turn out of the way a little, good Scholar, towards yonder high honeysuckle hedge: there we'll sit and sing whilst this shower falls so gently upon the teeming earth, and gives yet a sweeter smell to the lovely flowers that adorn these verdant meadows.

Look, under that broad Beech-tree, I sat down, when I was last this way a-fishing, and the birds in the adjoining grove seemed to have a friendly contention with an

Echo, whose dead voice seemed to live in a hollow cave, near to the brow of that Primrose-hill; there I sat viewing the silver streams glide silently towards their centre, the tempestuous sea; yet, sometimes opposed by rugged roots, and pebble stones, which broke their waves, and turned them into foam: and sometimes I beguiled time by viewing the harmless Lambs, some leaping securely in the cool shade, whilst others sported themselves in the cheerful Sun: and saw others were craving comfort from the swollen udders of their bleating Dams. As I thus sat, these and other sights had so fully possessed my soul with content, that I thought as the Poet has happily expressed it:

> I was for that time lifted above earth;
> And possessed joys not promised in my birth.

As I left this place, and entered into the next field, a second pleasure entertained me, 'twas a handsome Milkmaid that had not yet attained so much age and wisdom as to load her mind with any fears of many things that will never be (as too many men too often do), but she cast away all care, and sung like a Nightingale: her voice was good, and the Ditty fitted for it; 'twas that smooth song, which was made by Kit. Marlow, now at least fifty years ago: and the Milkmaid's Mother sung an answer to it, which was made by Sir Walter Rawleigh in his younger days.

They were old-fashioned Poetry, but choicely good, I think much better than the strong lines that are now in fashion in this critical age. Look yonder! on my word, yonder they both be a-milking again, I will give her the Chub, and persuade them to sing those two songs to us.

God speed you good woman, I have been a-fishing,

and am going to Bleak-Hall to my bed, and having caught more fish than will sup myself and my friend, I will bestow this upon you and your daughter, for I use to sell none.

John Earle

THE Character or Character-sketch, a description not of an individual but of a type, was a mode of writing common in the seventeenth century. Of all who practised it, John Earle (1601–65), Bishop of Salisbury, was one of the most expert and most famous; and of all his characters the one of a child, given here, is the best known. It exemplifies the observation, the tenderness, the thought, and the fancy which the good bishop possessed; though *Microcosmographie* first appeared in 1628, and Earle was not consecrated a bishop till 1662. After the seventeenth century Character-writing, as such, gradually passed out of fashion.

¶ A CHILD
From MICROCOSMOGRAPHIE

IS a Man in a small Letter, yet the best copy of *Adam* before he tasted of *Eve* or the apple; and he is happy whose small practice in the world can only write this Character. He is nature's fresh picture newly drawn in oil, which time, and much handling, dims and defaces. His Soul is yet a white paper unscribbled with observations of the world, wherewith, at length, it becomes a blurred notebook. He is purely happy, because he knows no evil, nor hath made means by sin to be acquainted with misery. He arrives not at the mischief of being wise, nor endures evils to come, by foreseeing them. He kisses and loves all, and, when the smart of the rod is past, smiles on his beater. Nature and his Parents alike dandle him, and 'tice him on with a bait of sugar to a draught of wormwood. He plays yet, like a young Prentice the first day, and is not come to his task of melancholy. All the language he speaks yet is tears, and they serve him well enough to express his necessity. His hardest labour is his tongue, as if he were loath to use so deceitful an Organ; and he is best company with it when he can but prattle. We laugh at his foolish sports, but his game is our earnest; and his drums, rattles, and hobby-horses, but the Emblems and mocking of man's business. His father hath writ him as his own little story, wherein he reads those days of his life that he cannot remember, and sighs to see what innocence he has out-lived. The elder he grows, he is a stair lower from God; and, like his first father, much worse in his breeches. He is the Christian's example, and the old man's relapse; the one imitates his pureness, and the other falls into his simplicity. Could he put off his body with his little coat, he had got eternity without a burthen, and exchanged but one Heaven for another.

Sir Thomas Browne

SIR THOMAS BROWNE (1605–82), was born in (of all unsuitable places) Cheapside. His father was a prosperous mercer and educated him at Winchester and Broadgates Hall (Pembroke College), Oxford.

He studied medicine at Oxford, Montpelier, Padua, and Leiden, and afterwards practised at Norwich. But he was by temperament a classical scholar and antiquary, loving best to read in dead languages of dead and dusty things. He had none of that scepticism and love of the inductive method which is said to be characteristic of the man from Missouri and the man of science; and he believed wholeheartedly in astrology, alchemy, and witchcraft.

He was a great writer in his own somewhat narrow vein: for he hit on one of the richest and most majestic styles in all literature, and through Coleridge, de Quincey, and Lamb had a lasting influence on English prose.

¶ PULVIS ET UMBRA SUMUS
From URN BURIAL

I

NOW since these dead bones have already outlasted the living ones of *Methuselah*, and in a Yard under Ground, and thin Walls of Clay, outworn all the strong and specious buildings above it, and quietly rested under the drums and tramplings of three Conquests; What Prince can promise such diuturnity unto his Relics, or might not gladly say,

Sic ego componi versus in ossa velim?

Time which antiquates Antiquities, and hath an art to make dust of all things, hath yet spared these *minor* Monuments. In vain we hope to be known by open and visible Conservatories, when to be unknown was the means of their continuation, and obscurity their protection.

II

What Song the *Syrens* sang, or what name *Achilles* assumed when he hid himself among Women, though puzzling Questions, are not beyond all conjecture. What time the Persons of these Ossuaries entered the *famous Nations of the dead*, and slept with Princes and Counsellors, might admit a wide solution. But who were the proprietaries of these bones, or what bodies these ashes made up, were a question above Antiquarism. Not to be resolved by Man not easily perhaps by

Spirits, except we consult the Provincial Guardians or Tutelary Observators. Had they made as good provision for their Names, as they have done for their Relics, they had not so grossly erred in the art of perpetuation. But to subsist in bones, and be but Pyramidally extant, is a fallacy in duration. Vain ashes, which in the oblivion of Names, Persons, Time, Sexes, have found unto themselves a fruitless continuation, and only arise unto late posterity as Emblems of mortal vanities; Antidotes against pride, vainglory, and maddening vices.

¶ THE HEROICK MIND
From CHRISTIAN MORALS

THE Heroical vein of Mankind runs much in the soldiery and courageous part of the World; and in that form we oftenest find men above men. History is full of the gallantry of that Tribe; and when we read their notable acts, we easily find what a difference there is between a life in *Plutarch* and in *Laertius*. Where true Fortitude dwells, Loyalty, Bounty, Friendship, and Fidelity may be found. A man may confide in persons constituted for noble ends, who dare do and suffer, and who have a hand to burn for their Country and their Friend. Small and creeping things are the product of petty Souls. He is like to be mistaken, who makes choice of a covetous Man for a Friend, or relieth upon the reed of narrow and poltron Friendship. Pitiful things are only to be found in the cottages of such Breasts; but bright Thoughts, clear Deeds, Constancy, Fidelity, Bounty, and generous Honesty are the Gems of noble Minds; wherein, to derogate from none, the true Heroick English Gentleman hath no Peer.

Thomas Fuller

THOMAS FULLER (1608-61), one of the most famous of English divines and historians, was born in a rectory and admitted to Cambridge at the age of 13. He was, it is said, 'a boy of pregnant wit', and he certainly was a B.A. by the time he was 17—if that is any evidence.

Receiving the curacy of St. Benet's, Cambridge, in 1630, he attracted attention by his quaint and humorous oratory. He turned his attention to letters, compiled *The Historie of the Holy Warre*, edited the *Worthies of England*, and made his fame secure with his *Church History of Britain*.

Fuller was a man of strong originality, sharp wit, and prodigious memory. He was also, as Coleridge has well said, 'incomparably the most sensible, the least prejudiced, great man of an age that boasted a galaxy of great men'.

¶ WYCLIFFE'S ASHES
From CHURCH HISTORY OF BRITAIN

HITHERTO the corpse of John Wickliffe had quietly slept in his grave about one and forty years after his death, till his body was reduced to bones and his bones almost to dust.... But now such the Spleen of the Council of Constance... as they ordered his bones (with this charitable caution, if it may be discerned from the bodies of other faithful people) to be taken out of the ground and thrown farre off from any Christian buriall. In obedience hereunto Richard Fleming Bishop of Lincolne Diocesan of Lutterworth sent his officers... to ungrave him accordingly. To Lutterworth they come, Sumner, Commissary Official, Chancellor, Proctors, Doctors, and the Servants (so that the Remnant of the body would not hold out a bone amongst so many hands) take what was left out of the grave, and burnt them to ashes, and cast them into Swift a neighbouring Brook running hard by. Thus this Brook hath convey'd his Ashes into Avon; Avon into Severn; Severn into the narrow Seas; they, into the main Ocean. And thus the Ashes of Wickliff are the Emblem of his Doctrine, which now is dispersed all the World over.

John Milton

JOHN MILTON (1608–74), the greatest of English non-dramatic poets, was a prominent figure on the Puritan side in the Civil Wars, and Latin Secretary to the Council of State under Oliver Cromwell, Latin being still the language of diplomacy. After Dante he is the most learned of poets, and his *Paradise Lost* did for Puritanism what Dante's *Commedia* did for Catholicism. But this and his other great writings are much more—they are the expression of an extreme endurance and a noble hope. In prose his chief English work was the *Areopagitica*, a defence of the freedom of the Press.

¶ THE TYRANNY OF LICENSING
From AREOPAGITICA

IF we think to regulate Printing, thereby to rectify manners, we must regulate all recreations and pastimes, all that is delightful to man. No musick must be heard, no song be set or sung, but what is grave and *Dorick*. There must be licensing dancers, that no gesture, motion, or deportment be taught our youth but what by their allowance shall be thought honest; for such *Plato* was provided of. It will ask more than the work of twenty licencers to examine all the lutes, the violins, and the guitars in every house; they must not be suffered to prattle as they do, but must be licensed what they may say. And who shall silence all the airs and madrigals that whisper softness in chambers? The Windows also, and the *Balconies* must be thought on: there are shrewd books with dangerous Frontispieces set to sale; who shall prohibit them? shall twenty licencers? The villages also must have their visitors to inquire what lectures the bagpipe and the rebeck reads, even to the balladry and the gamut of every *municipal* fiddler, for these are the Countryman's *Arcadia*'s and his *Monte Mayors*. . . . To sequester out of the world into *Atlantick* and *Eutopian* polities, which never can be drawn into use, will not mend our condition; but to ordain wisely as in this world of evil, in the midst whereof God hath placed us unavoidably.

Edward Hyde

EDWARD HYDE (1609–74) was one of the very few Englishmen who have both made history and written it. Under Charles I he was the most moderate of the Royalist leaders; he did more than any other man to make the Restoration possible, and for the first eight years of Charles II he practically ruled England as Lord Chancellor. His *History of the Great Rebellion* is both a masterpiece of narrative prose and an authority of the first rank for the period, and especially for the personalities, with which it deals.

¶ CHARACTER OF LORD FALKLAND

From A HISTORY OF THE REBELLION

As he was of a most incomparable gentleness, application, and even a demissness and submission to good, and worthy, and entire Men, so he was naturally (which could not but be more evident in his Place, which objected him to another conversation and intermixture, than his own election had done) *adversus malos injucundus*; and was so ill a dissembler of his dislike and disinclination to ill Men, that it was not possible for Such not to discern it. There was once, in the House of Commons, such a declared acceptation of the good Service an eminent Member had done to them, and, as they said, to the whole Kingdom, that it was moved, he being present, 'that the Speaker might, in the name of the whole House, give him thanks; and then, that every Member might, as a testimony of his particular acknowledgement, stir or move his hat towards him'; the which (though not ordered) when very many did, the Lord Falkland (who believed the Service itself not to be of that moment, and that an honorable and generous Person could not have stooped to it for any recompence) instead of moving his hat, stretched both his Arms out, and clasped his hands together upon the crown of his hat, and held it close down to his head; that all Men might see how odious that flattery was to him, and the very approbation of the Person, though at that time most popular.

When there was any Overture, or hope of Peace, he would be more erect and vigorous, and exceedingly sollicitous to press anything which he thought might promote it; and sitting amongst his Friends, often, after a deep silence and frequent sighs, would, with a shrill and sad accent, ingeminate the word *Peace, Peace*; and would passionately profess 'that the very agony of the War, and the view of the calamities and desolation the Kingdom did, and must endure, took his sleep from him, and would shortly break his heart.' This made some think, or pretend to think, 'that he was so much enamoured on Peace, that he would have been glad, the King should have bought it at any price,' which was a most unreasonable Calumny. As if a Man that was himself the most punctual and precise in every circumstance that might reflect upon Conscience or Honour, could have wished the King to have committed a trespass against either.

Old Testament

THESE selections are from the Bible—that storehouse of much of the richest, most magnificent, and (in the literary as well as religious sense) most truly inspired prose ever written.

Amid all the glories of the Scriptures it is hard to pick and choose; but no one will quarrel with the selection of these passages from Isaiah, the Hebrew prophet, who seems to have spent his life in Jerusalem in the eighth century B.C. For eloquence, fire, and the authentic note of prophecy, Isaiah is equalled only by the greatest of the other Old Testament writers.

I

¶ 'THINE EYES SHALL SEE THE KING IN HIS BEAUTY'

From ISAIAH xxxiii. 17–24

THINE eyes shall see the king in his beauty: they shall behold the land that is very far off. Thine heart shall meditate terror. Where is the scribe? Where is the receiver? Where is he that counted the towers? Thou shalt not see a fierce people, a people of a deeper speech than thou canst perceive; of a stammering tongue, that thou canst not understand. Look upon Zion, the city of our solemnities: thine eyes shall see Jerusalem a quiet habitation, a tabernacle that shall not be taken down, not one of the stakes thereof shall ever be removed, neither shall any of the cords thereof be broken. But there the glorious Lord will be unto us a place of broad rivers and streams; wherein shall go no galley with oars, neither shall gallant ship pass thereby. For the Lord is our judge, the Lord is our lawgiver, the Lord is our king,

He will save us. Thy tacklings are loosed; they could not well strengthen their mast, they could not spread the sail; then is the prey of a great spoil divided, the lame take the prey. And the inhabitant shall not say: I am sick: the people that dwell therein shall be forgiven their iniquity.

II

¶ 'ARISE, SHINE'
From ISAIAH lx. 1–3, 19–20

ARISE, shine; for thy light is come, and the glory of the Lord is risen upon thee. For, behold, the darkness shall cover the earth, and gross darkness the people; but the Lord shall arise upon thee, and His glory shall be seen upon thee. And the Gentiles shall come to thy light, and kings to the brightness of thy rising. The sun shall be no more thy light by day, neither for brightness shall the moon give light unto thee; but the Lord shall be unto thee an everlasting light, and thy God thy glory. Thy sun shall no more go down, neither shall thy moon withdraw itself; for the Lord shall be thine everlasting light, and the days of thy mourning shall be ended.

III

¶ 'REMEMBER NOW THY CREATOR'
From ECCLESIASTES xii

REMEMBER now thy Creator in the days of thy youth, while the evil days come not, nor the years draw nigh, when thou shalt say, I have no pleasure in them; while the sun, or the light, or the moon, or the stars, be not darkened, nor the clouds return after the rain: In the day when the keepers of the house shall tremble, and the strong men shall bow themselves, and the grinders cease because they are few, and those that look out of the windows be darkened. And the doors shall be shut in the streets, when the sound of the grinding is low, and he shall rise up at the voice of the bird, and all the daughters of musick shall be brought low; also when they shall be afraid of that which is high, and fears shall be in the way, and the almond tree shall flourish, and the grasshopper shall be a burden, and desire shall fail: because man goeth to his long home, and the mourners go about the streets: or ever the silver cord be loosed, or the golden bowl be broken, or the pitcher be broken at the fountain, or the wheel broken at the cistern. Then shall the dust return to the earth as it was: and the spirit shall return unto God who gave it. Vanity of vanities, saith the preacher; all is vanity. And moreover, because the preacher was wise, he still taught the people knowledge; yea, he gave good heed, and sought out, and set in order many proverbs. The preacher sought to find out acceptable words: and that which was written was upright, even words of truth. The words of the wise are as goads, and as nails fastened by the masters of assemblies, which are given from one shepherd. And further, by these, my son, be admonished: of making many books there is no end; and much study is a weariness of the flesh. Let us hear the conclusion of the whole matter: Fear God, and keep his commandments: for this is the whole duty of man. For God shall bring every work into judgment, with every secret thing, whether it be good, or whether it be evil.

IV
¶ 'THE VOICE OF MY BELOVED!'
From SONG OF SOLOMON ii. 8–17; v. 2–8

(i)

THE voice of my beloved! behold, he cometh leaping upon the mountains, skipping upon the hills.

My beloved is like a roe or a young hart: behold, he standeth behind our wall, he looketh forth at the windows, shewing himself through the lattice.

My beloved spake, and said unto me, Rise up, my love, my fair one, and come away.

For, lo, the winter is past, the rain is over and gone.

The flowers appear on the earth; the time of the singing of birds is come, and the voice of the turtle is heard in our land.

The fig tree putteth forth her green figs, and the vines with the tender grape give a good smell. Arise, my love, my fair one, and come away.

O my dove, that art in the clefts of the rock, in the secret places of the stairs, let me see thy countenance, let me hear thy voice; for sweet is thy voice, and thy countenance is comely.

Take us the foxes, the little foxes, that spoil the vines: for our vines have tender grapes.

My beloved is mine, and I am his: he feedeth among the lilies.

Until the day break, and the shadows flee away, turn, my beloved, and be thou like a roe or a young hart upon the mountains of Bether.

(ii)

I sleep, but my heart waketh: it is the voice of my beloved that knocketh, saying, Open to me, my sister, my love, my dove, my undefiled: for my head is filled with dew, and my locks with the drops of the night.

I have put off my coat; how shall I put it on? I have washed my feet; how shall I defile them?

My beloved put in his hand by the hole of the door, and my bowels were moved for him.

I rose up to open to my beloved; and my hands dropped with myrrh, and my fingers with sweet smelling myrrh, upon the handles of the lock.

I opened to my beloved; but my beloved had withdrawn himself, and was gone; my soul failed when he spake: I sought him, but I could not find him; I called him, but he gave me no answer.

The watchmen that went about the city found me, they smote me, they wounded me; the keepers of the walls took away my veil from me.

I charge you, O daughters of Jerusalem, if ye find my beloved, that ye tell him, that I am sick of love.

New Testament
¶ ST. PAUL ON DEATH
From I CORINTHIANS xv. 51–end

'IT is probable', a biographer has said, 'that no man ever swayed the religious opinions and destinies of mankind as powerfully as did Paul of Tarsus, the Apostle of the Gentiles. He was greater than the greatest servants of Christ in many single capacities; a greater preacher than Chrysostom, a greater missionary than St. Francis Xavier, a greater theologian than St. Thomas of Aquinum, a greater reformer than Luther, a greater organiser than St. Gregory the Great.... The secrets of his unparalleled success were—regarded on the human side—burning zeal, absolute self-sacrifice, undaunted courage and a strong conviction that he was fulfilling a ministry to which he had received a special call from God.'

The biographer might have added the qualities without which

St. Paul's letters would have been valued only by the zealous—his fiery eloquence and supreme style. Both qualities are manifested in the following passage from his great Epistle to the Corinthians.

BEHOLD, I show you a mystery: We shall not all sleep, but we shall all be changed, in a moment, in the twinkling of an eye, at the last trump: for the trumpet shall sound, and the dead shall be raised incorruptible, and we shall be changed. For this corruptible must put on incorruption, and this mortal must put on immortality. So when this corruptible shall have put on incorruption, and this mortal shall have put on immortality, then shall be brought to pass the saying that is written, Death is swallowed up in victory. O death, where is thy sting? O grave, where is thy victory? The sting of death is sin; and the strength of sin is the law. But thanks be to God, which giveth us the victory through our Lord Jesus Christ. Therefore, my beloved brethren, be ye stedfast, unmoveable, always abounding in the work of the Lord, forasmuch as ye know that your labour is not in vain in the Lord.

The Apocrypha

THIS selection is one of the most famous passages from the Apocrypha.

¶ 'GOD'S PURPOSE IS ETERNAL'
From 2 ESDRAS vi. 1–6

AND he said unto me, in the beginning, when the earth was made, before the borders of the world stood, or ever the winds blew, before it thundered and lightened, or ever the foundations of Paradise were laid, before the fair flowers were seen, or ever the moveable powers were established, before the innumerable multitude of angels were gathered together, or ever the heights of the air were lifted up, before the measures of the firmament were named, or ever the chimneys in Sion were hot, and ere the present years were sought out, and or ever the inventions of them that now sin were turned, before they were sealed that have gathered faith for a treasure: Then did I consider these things, and they all were made through me alone, and through none other: by me also they shall be ended, and by none other.

The English Liturgy

THESE three collects come from what is called the First Prayer Book of Edward VI, issued in 1549. The first was a translation from the old Sarum Missal; the other two were composed in 1549, possibly by Thomas Cranmer, Archbishop of Canterbury.

¶ COLLECTS FROM THE FIRST PRAYER BOOK OF EDWARD VI

i. FOURTH SUNDAY AFTER EASTER

ALMIGHTIE God, whiche doest make the myndes of all faythfull men to be of one wil: graunt unto thy people, that they maye loue the thyng, whiche thou commaundest, and desyre that whiche thou doest promes, that emong the sondery and manifold chaunges of the worlde, oure heartes maye surely there bee fixed, whereas true ioyes are to be founde: through Christe our Lorde.

ii. ALL SAINTS' DAY

ALMIGHTIE God, whiche haste knitte together thy electe in one communion and felowship in the misticall body of thy sonne Christe our Lord; graunt us grace so to folow thy holy Saynctes in all virtues, and godly liuyng, that we maye come to those unspeakeable ioyes, whiche thou hast prepared for all them that unfaynedly loue thee; through Jesus Christe.

iii. COLLECT FROM THE COMMUNION OFFICE

ALMIGHTIE God, the fountayn of all wisdome, which knowest our necessities beefore we aske, and our ignoraunce in asking: we besehe thee to haue compassion upon our infirmities, and those thynges, whiche for our unwoorthines we dare not, and for our blindnes we cannot aske, vouchsaue to geue us for the woorthines of thy sonne Jesu Christ our Lorde. Amen.

John Holland

JOHN HOLLOND (or Holland) entered the King's service in or about 1624 as a clerk. He became paymaster of the Navy some ten years later. In 1636 he was accused of corruption, but pleaded that this had been permissible for 30 years, and, though the practice was abolished by an Order in Council, he was not specially punished.

His *First Discourse of the Navy* was described by Sir William Penn as 'writ by an able hand ... and most fit to be read'. But Penn has proved an optimist: precious few people these days have even heard of Hollond, let alone read a line of him.

¶ A DISCOURSE OF THE NAVY
From FIRST DISCOURSE OF THE NAVY

IF either the honour of a nation, commerce or trade with all nations, peace at home, grounded upon our enemies' fear or love of us abroad, and attended with plenty of all things necessary either for the preservation of the public weal or thy private welfare, be things worthy thy esteem (though it may be beyond thy shoal conceit), then next to God and the King give thy thanks for the same to the navy, as the principal instrument whereby God works these good things to thee.

As for honour, who knows not (that knows anything) that in all records of late times of actions chronicled to the everlasting fame and renown of this kingdom, still the naval part is the thread that runs through the whole wooft, the burden of the song, the scope of the text? that whereby Queen Elizabeth of famous memory immortalised her name by her many great victories obtained over all her enemies, neighbours or remote dwellers; King James of ever blessed memory by almost silent commands commanded the silence, if not the love, of all neighbouring nations; and that whereby our ever blessed Charles, when his abused patience began to be slighted (as that his power on the seas and right to the seas began thereby to be questioned), hath not only by his late expeditions of 1635, 1636, 1637, and 1638, quelled foreign insolencies, regained our almost lost power and honour, silenced home-bred malcontents, but also settled his kingdoms in peace, commerce, and plenty, the common attendants of so wise and honourable a government?

Whence is it that sundry nations that are enemies amongst themselves are all friends to the English? that we can, and do, convoy all French and Dutch bottoms to their several ports, and protect them from the fear and annoyance of the Spanish party; and on the contrary, all Spanish and Dunkirk bottoms to their several ports, and protect them from the encounter of the French and Dutch parties? How comes it to pass that when both parties are under the tuition of any of his Majesty's castles or ships, neither party dare disturb the quiet of each other till they be both out of protection? ...

I could instance in many more particulars, were it not to prove it day at noon; suffice it thus far, nothing under God, who doth all, hath brought so much, so great commerce to this kingdom as the rightly noble employments of our navy; a wheel, if truly turned, that sets to work all Christendom by its motion; a mill, if well extended, that in a sweet yet sovereign composure contracts the grist of all nations to its own dominions, and requires only the tribute of its own people, not for, but towards, its maintenance.

Jeremy Taylor

JEREMY TAYLOR (1613–67) was the most eloquent of the High Church divines who enjoyed the patronage of Archbishop Laud. In his day he was most famous as a pamphleteer on behalf of the Episcopalian and Royalist cause, but it is his sermons which are now read. The following is taken from them.

¶ AGAINST BITTERNESS OF ZEAL
From SERMONS

ANY Zeal is proper for Religion, but the zeal of the Sword and the Zeal of Anger; this is the Bitterness of Zeal, and it is a certain Temptation to every Man against his Duty; for if the Sword turns Preacher, and dictates Propositions by Empire instead of Arguments, and engraves them in Men's Hearts with a Poignard, that it shall be Death to believe what I innocently and ignorantly am persuaded of, it must needs be unsafe to try the Spirits, to try all Things, to make inquiry; and yet, without this Liberty, no Man can justify himself before God or Man, nor confidently say that his Religion is best; since he cannot without a final Danger make himself to give a right Sentence, and to follow that which he finds to be best. This may ruin Souls by making Hypocrites, or careless and compliant against Conscience or without it; but it does not save Souls, though peradventure it should force them to a good Opinion. This is Inordination of Zeal; for Christ, by reproving St. Peter drawing his Sword even in the Cause of Christ, for his sacred and yet injured Person, saith Theophylact, 'teaches us not to use the Sword, though in the cause of God or for God himself.' . . .

When Abraham sat at his Tent Door, according to his custom, waiting to entertain Strangers, he espied an old Man, stooping and leaning on his Staff, weary with Age and Travel, coming towards him, who was a hundred years of Age. He received him kindly, washed his Feet, provided Supper, caused him to sit down; but observing that the Old man Eat and prayed not, nor begged a Blessing on his Meat, he asked him why he did not worship the God of Heaven. The old man told him that he worshipped the Fire only, and acknowledged no other God. At which answer Abraham grew so zealously angry that he thrust the old Man out of his Tent, and exposed him to all the Evils of the Night and an unguarded Condition. When the old Man was gone, God called to Abraham and asked him where the Stranger was? He replied, I thrust him away because he did not worship thee. God answered him, 'I have suffered him these hundred Years, although he dishonoured me; and couldst not thou endure him one Night?'

John Bunyan

JOHN BUNYAN (1628–88), tinker, prisoner, and Christian, passed through a long process of conversion between the ages of twenty and twenty-four, and was imprisoned (rather less than more strictly) in Bedford Jail for unlicensed preaching 1660–72. *The Pilgrim's Progress from this World to that which is to come*, published in 1678, is one of the great literary and spiritual classics of English prose. It is one of the very few books that have been able to make religion (whether disguised in an allegory or obvious in a discussion) exciting and realistic. It is of course one-sided in its theology (Bunyan was no tolerant Puritan), but it is so 'human at the red-ripe of the heart' that its battles are thrilling for small boys and its prophecies almost credible by the adult.

¶ THE VALLEY OF HUMILIATION
From THE PILGRIM'S PROGRESS

BUT we will come again to this Valley of *Humiliation*. It is the best, and most fruitful piece of Ground in all those parts. It is fat Ground, and as you see consisteth much in Meadows; and if a Man was to come here in the Summer-time as we do now, if he knew not anything before thereof, and if he also delighted himself in the sight of his Eyes, he might see that that would be delightful to him. Behold, how green this Valley is, also how beautified with *Lilies*. I have also known many labouring men that have got good Estates in this Valley of *Humiliation*. (For God resisteth the Proud; but gives *more, more* Grace to the Humble) for indeed it is a very fruitful Soil, and doth bring forth by handfuls. Some also have wished that the next way to their Father's House were here, that they might be troubled no more with either Hills or Mountains to go over; but the way is the way, and there's an end.

Now as they were going along and talking, they

espied a Boy feeding his Father's Sheep. The Boy was in very mean Cloathes, but of a very fresh and well-favoured Countenance, and as he sat by himself he sung. Hark, said Mr. *Greatheart*, to what the Shepherd's Boy saith. So they hearkened, and he said,

> *He that is down, needs fear no fall,*
> *He that is low, no Pride:*
> *He that is humble, ever shall*
> *Have God to be his Guide.*
>
> *I am content with what I have,*
> *Little be it, or much:*
> *And, Lord, contentment still I crave,*
> *Because thou savest such.*
>
> *Fullness to such a burden is*
> *That go on Pilgrimage:*
> *Here little, and hereafter Bliss,*
> *Is best from Age to Age.*

Then said the *Guide*, Do you hear him? I will dare to say, that this Boy lives a merrier Life, and wears more of that Herb called *Hearts-ease* in his Bosom, than he that is clad in Silk and Velvet; but we will proceed in our Discourse.

¶ MR. VALIANT-FOR-TRUTH CROSSES THE RIVER

From THE PILGRIM'S PROGRESS

AFTER this, it was noised abroad that Mr. *Valiant-for-truth* was taken with a Summons, by the same *Post* as the other, and had this for a Token that the Summons was true, *That his Pitcher was broken at the Fountain.* When he understood it, he called for his Friends, and told them of it. Then said he, I am going to my Father's, and though with great difficulty I am got hither, yet now I do not repent me of all the Trouble I have been at to arrive where I am. *My Sword*, I give to him that shall succeed me in my Pilgrimage, and my *Courage* and *Skill*, to him that can get it. My *Marks* and *Scars* I carry with me, to be a Witness for me, that I have fought his Battles who now will be my Rewarder. When the Day that he must go hence, was come, many accompanied him to the River side, into which, as he went, he said, *Death, where is thy Sting?* And as he went down deeper, he said, *Grave, where is thy Victory?* So he passed over, and the Trumpets sounded for him on the other side.

John Dryden

JOHN DRYDEN (1631–1700), himself a noble praiser, has been nobly praised and with justice. He was the first Poet Laureate definitely so appointed by patent (in 1670). He was one of the first who brought the wild muses of the earlier poets of his century back to civilization, argument, and the town. He was one of the great masters of a direct and simple prose. 'Nothing', Johnson wrote of it, 'is cold or languid; the whole is airy, animated, and vigorous; what is little is gay; what is great, is splendid'. . . . 'always equable and always varied'.

Dryden's career in literature was notable. He began with poetry and passed on to plays, as a result of which the *Essay on Dramatic Poesy*, defending the use of rhyme in tragedy, was written. The four persons mentioned in the extract below, of whose discussion the essay purports to be an account, are, respectively, Lord Buckhurst, Sir Robert Howard (Dryden's chief opponent), Sir Charles Sedley, and Dryden himself. The controversy lasted longer but this was its chief product. He proceeded to increase his reputation in all three mediums, and his critical writings are the most admirable in English literature before Johnson.

¶ JUNE 3RD, 1665
From ESSAY OF DRAMATIC POESY

IT was that memorable day, in the first summer of the late War, when our Navy engaged the Dutch; a day wherein the two most mighty and best-appointed Fleets which any age had ever seen, disputed the command of the greater half of the Globe, the commerce of nations, and the riches of the Universe. While these vast floating bodies, on either side, moved against each other in parallel lines, and our Countrymen, under the happy conduct of his Royal Highness, went breaking, by little and little, into the line of the Enemies; the noise of the Cannon from both Navies reached our ears about the City, so that all men being alarmed with it, and in a dreadful suspense of the event which we knew was then deciding, every one went following the sound as his fancy led him; and leaving the Town almost empty, some took towards the Park, some cross the River, others down it; all seeking the noise in the depth of silence.

Among the rest it was the fortune of *Eugenius*, *Crites*, *Lisideius*, and *Neander*, to be in company together; three of them persons whom their wit and Quality have made known to all the Town; and whom I have chose to hide under these borrowed names that they may not suffer by so ill a relation as I am going to make of their discourse.

Taking then a Barge which a servant of *Lisideius* had provided for them, they made haste to shoot the Bridge, and left behind them that great fall of waters which hindered them from hearing what they desired: after which, having disengaged themselves from many

Vessels which rode at anchor in the *Thames* and almost blocked up the passage towards *Greenwich*, they ordered the Watermen to let fall their oars more gently; and then, every one favouring his own curiosity with a strict silence, it was not long ere they perceived the Air break about them like the noise of distant Thunder, or of swallows in a Chimney: those little undulations of sound, though almost vanishing before they reached them, yet still seeming to retain somewhat of their first horror which they had betwixt the Fleets. After they had attentively listened till such time as the sound by little and little went from them, *Eugenius*, lifting up his head, and taking notice of it, was the first who congratulated to the rest that happy Omen of our Nation's Victory: adding, we had but this to desire in confirmation of it, that we might hear no more of that noise which was now leaving the English Coast.

The Marquess of Halifax

THIS selection is from the works of a man little read nowadays, great personage though he was in his day.

George Savile, first Marquess of Halifax (1633-95), one of the foremost statesmen, writers, and thinkers of his time, was the son of a Yorkshire baronet and a connexion of Shaftesbury and other influential men.

He entered Parliament in 1660, first became really prominent in 1667, when he was made Viscount Halifax, and won a high reputation as a diplomat and member of the Privy Council and House of Lords. He became one of the King's chief advisers in 1679, and it was largely owing to his efforts that the Exclusion Bill, designed to shut out James from the throne, was rejected.

But he was never friendly with James, opposed all his unconstitutional acts, and ultimately joined William of Orange. He called himself a 'Trimmer'; was called by others (more bluntly and less justly) a turncoat; and strove always for compromise and moderation. He was a clear and able thinker and a brilliant wit.

His most famous book is *The Character of a Trimmer*. He also left a number of treatises on practical statecraft, from one of which this passage is taken.

¶ LOOK TO YOUR MOAT
From A ROUGH DRAFT OF A NEW MODEL AT SEA

I WILL make no other Introduction to the following Discourse, than that as the Importance of our being strong at Sea was ever very great, so in our present Circumstances it is grown to be much greater; because, as formerly our Force in Shipping contributed greatly to our Trade and Safety, so now it is become indispensably necessary to our very being.

It may be said now to England, Martha, Martha, *thou art busy about many things, but one thing* is necessary. To the question, What shall we do to be saved in this World? there is no other answer but this, Look to your *Moat*.

The first Article of an Englishman's Political Creed must be, That he believeth in the Sea, &c., without that there needeth no General Council to pronounce him incapable of Salvation here.

We are in an Island, confined to it by God Almighty, not as a Penalty but a Grace, and one of the greatest that can be given to Mankind. Happy confinement, that hath made us Free, Rich, and Quiet; a fair Portion in this World, and very well worth the preserving; a Figure that ever hath been envied, and could never be imitated by our Neighbours. Our Situation hath made Greatness abroad by Land Conquests unnatural things to us. It is true, we have made Excursions, and glorious ones too, which make our Names great in history but they did not last.

Samuel Pepys

SAMUEL PEPYS (1633–1703) was 'clerk of the king's ships', an efficient Admiralty administrator, and a hard-working Civil servant. But his more apparent importance—since the first deciphering of his Diary in 1825—has been in the intimate and perfect presentation to us of his whole mind and nature. His interest in detail which helped to make him a success in his office combines here with an interest in himself and in others to present a panorama of the world in which he moved and of his emotions as he moved through it. It is his fantastic genius for putting everything down—as, for example, below 'and particularly of the pride and ignorance of Mrs. Lowther'—which distinguish him from the ordinary business man; that, and his intense interest in art and life. The diary, because of his failing eyesight, was discontinued on 31 May 1669; to do so was 'almost as much as to see himself go into his grave'.

¶ A JAUNT INTO THE COUNTRY
From HIS DIARY

JULY 14, 1667. (Lord's day.) Up, and my wife, a little before four, and to make us ready; and by and by Mrs. Turner come to us by agreement, and she and I stayed talking below while my wife dressed herself, which vexed me that she was so long about it, keeping us till past five o'clock before she was ready. She ready; and taking some bottles of wine, and beer, and some cold fowl with us into the coach, we took coach and four horses, which I had provided last night, and so away. A very fine day, and so towards Epsom, talking all the way pleasantly, and particularly of the pride and ignorance of Mrs. Lowther, in having of her train carried up. The country very fine, only the way very dusty. To Epsom, by eight o'clock, to the well; where much company, and I drank the water: they did not, but I did drink four pints. And to the town, to the King's Head; and hear that my Lord Buckhurst and Nelly are lodged at the next house, and Sir Charles Sedley with them; and keep a merry house. Poor girl! I pity her; but more the loss of her at the King's house. W. Hewer rode with us, and I left him and the women, and myself walked to church, where few people to what I expected, and none I knew, but all the Houblons, brothers, and them after sermon I did salute, and walk with towards my inn. James did tell me that I was the only happy man of the Navy, of whom, he says, during all this freedom the people hath taken to speaking treason, he hath not heard one bad word of me, which is a great joy to me; for I hear the same of others, but do know that I have deserved as well as most. We parted to meet anon, and I to my women into a better room, which the people of the house borrowed for us, and there to a good dinner, and were merry, and Pembleton come to us, who happened to be in the house, and there talked and were merry.

After dinner, he gone, we all lay down (the day being wonderful hot) to sleep, and each of us took a good nap, and then rose . . . and we took coach and to take the air, there being a fine breeze abroad; and I carried them to the well, and there filled some bottles of water to carry home with me; and there I talked with the two women that farm the well, at £12 per annum, of the lord of the manor . . . Here W. Hewer's horse broke loose, and we had the sport to see him taken again. Then I carried them to see my cousin Pepys's house, and 'light, and walked round about it, and they like it, as indeed it deserves, very well, and is a pretty place; and then I walked them to the wood hard by, and there got them in the thickets till they lost themselves, and

I could not find the way into any of the walks in the wood, which indeed are very pleasant, if I could have found them. At last got out of the wood again; and I, by leaping down the little bank, coming out of the wood, did sprain my right foot, which brought me great present pain, but presently, with walking, it went away for the present, and so the women and W. Hewer and I walked upon the Downes, where a flock of sheep was; and the most pleasant and innocent sight that ever I saw in my life. We found a shepherd and his little boy reading, far from any houses or sight of people, the Bible to him; so I made the boy read to me, which he did, with the forced tone that children do usually read, that was mighty pretty, and then I did give him something, and went to the father, and talked with him; and I find he had been a servant in my cousin Pepys's house, and told me what was become of their old servants. He did content himself mightily in my liking his boy's reading, and did bless God for him, the most like one of the old patriarchs that ever I saw in my life, and it brought those thoughts of the old age of the world in my mind for two or three days after. We took notice of his woollen knit stockings of two colours mixed, and of his shoes shod with iron, both at the toe and heels, and with great nails in the soles of his feet, which was mighty pretty; and, taking notice of them, 'why,' says the poor man, 'the downes, you see, are full of stones, and we are fain to shoe ourselves thus; and these', says he, 'will make the stones fly till they ring before me.' I did give the poor man something, for which he was mighty thankful, and I tried to cast stones with his horn crook. He values his dog mightily, that would turn a sheep any way which he would have him, when he goes to fold them:

told me there was about eighteen score sheep in his flock, and that he hath four shillings a-week the year round for keeping of them: and Mrs. Turner, in the common fields here, did gather one of the prettiest nosegays that ever I saw in my life.

So to our coach, and through Mr. Minnes's wood, and looked upon Mr. Evelyn's house; and so over the common, and through Epsom town to our inn, in the way stopping a poor woman with her milk-pail, and in one of my gilt tumblers did drink our bellyfuls of milk, better than any cream; and so to our inn, and there had a dish of cream, but it was sour, and so had no pleasure in it; and so paid our reckoning, and took coach, it being about seven at night, and passed and saw the people walking with their wives and children to take the air, and we set out for home, the sun by and by going down, and we in the cool of the evening all the way with much pleasure home, talking and pleasing ourselves with the pleasure of this day's work. Mrs. Turner mightily pleased with my resolution, which, I tell her, is never to keep a country-house, but to keep a coach, and with my wife on the Saturday to go sometimes for a day to this place, and then quit to another place; and there is more variety and as little charge, and no trouble, as there is in a country-house. Anon it grew dark, and we had the pleasure to see several glow-worms, which was mighty pretty, but my foot begins more and more to pain me, which Mrs. Turner, by keeping her warm hand upon it, did much ease: but so that when we come home, which was just at eleven at night, I was not able to walk from the lane's end to my house without being helped. So to bed, and there had a cere-cloth laid to my foot, but in great pain all night long.

Thomas Traherne

THOMAS TRAHERNE (1636–74), the son of a Hereford shoemaker, went from Oxford into the Church and contrived to live an uneventful life amid all the turmoil of his time. While others intrigued and fought he meditated in his country parsonage. And his style is the man: earnest, contemplative, and serene. It has nevertheless an occasional ecstasy, and moments of realization which approach near to authentic mystical knowledge.

Traherne was also a poet, but is best known by his *Centuries of Meditations*, the MSS. of which were discovered by accident on a bookstall more than 200 years after his death, and published in 1903. The following is characteristic of his style.

¶ THE HEIR OF ALL THINGS
From CENTURIES OF MEDITATIONS

YOU never enjoy the world aright, till the Sea itself floweth in your veins, till you are clothed with the heavens, and crowned with the stars: and perceive yourself to be the sole heir of the whole world, and more than so, because men are in it who are every one sole heirs as well as you. Till you can sing and rejoice and delight in God, as misers do in gold, and Kings in sceptres, you never enjoy the world.

Till your spirit filleth the whole world, and the stars are your jewels; till you are as familiar with the ways of God in all Ages as with your walk and table: till you are intimately acquainted with that shady nothing out of which the world was made: till you love men so as to desire their happiness with a thirst equal to the zeal of your own: till you delight in God for being good to all: you never enjoy the world. Till you more feel it than your private estate, and are more present in the hemisphere, considering the glories and the beauties there, than in your own house: Till you remember how lately you were made, and how wonderful it was when you came into it: and more rejoice in the palace of your glory, than if it had been made but to-day morning.

Daniel Defoe

DANIEL DEFOE (*c.* 1659–1731) was the son of a butcher in St. Giles named James Foe. As a first sign of genius he changed his name to Defoe. Next he abandoned the clothing and brick-making trades in favour of the sword, taking part in the Duke of Monmouth's rebellion and fighting for William III.

And then he took to politics, visited the Continent, scribbled dissenting and other pamphlets, got himself twice into Newgate and three times into the pillory, was much harassed in his early days by creditors, and died in 1731 at Ropemakers' Alley, Moorfields, where he had been living in obscurity.

Of all Defoe's 375 publications only a few are read to-day—his novels *Moll Flanders* (1721), *Colonel Jacque* (1722), and *Roxana* (1724), his graphic *Journal of the Plague Year* (1722), and, of course, the immortal *Robinson Crusoe*.

¶ THE FOOTPRINT

From ROBINSON CRUSOE

IT happened one day about noon, going towards my boat, I was exceedingly surprised with the print of a man's naked foot on the shore, which was very plain to be seen in the sand.

I stood like one thunderstruck, or as if I had seen an apparition. I listened, I looked round me, I could hear nothing nor see anything. I went up to a rising ground, to look farther. I went up the shore, and down the shore, but it was all one; I could see no other impression but that one. I went to it again to see if there were any more, and to observe if it might not be my fancy; but there was no room for that, for there was exactly the very print of a foot—toes, heel, and every part of a foot.

How it came thither I knew not, nor could in the least imagine. But after innumerable fluttering thoughts, like a man perfectly confused and out of myself, I came home to my fortification, not feeling, as we say, the ground I went on, but terrified to the last degree, looking behind me at every two or three steps, mistaking every bush and tree, and fancying every stump at a distance to be a man: nor is it possible to describe how many various shapes affrighted imagination represented things to me in, how many wild ideas were found every moment in my fancy, and what strange, unaccountable whimsies came into my thoughts by the way.

When I came to my castle, for so I think I called it ever after this, I fled into it like one pursued. Whether I went over by the ladder, as first contrived, or went in at the hole in the rock, which I called a door, I cannot remember; no, nor could I remember the next morning, for never frighted hare fled to cover, or fox to earth, with more terror of mind than I to this retreat.

Jonathan Swift

JONATHAN SWIFT (1667–1745) is one of the greatest writers of English prose, and a by no means negligible poet. He came to England from Ireland in 1688, and after twenty-six years among statesmen, courtiers, poets, and journalists, was compelled to return in 1714 with no more preferment than that of the Deanery of St. Patrick's. His prose has no tricks and hardly any characteristics except simplicity, but that simplicity is a perfect means for irony, anger, horror, and an unsatisfied passion for beauty and righteousness to express themselves. His most famous book, *Gulliver's Travels*, from which the second extract is taken, is an amusing story but also a profound 'criticism of life'.

¶ A STANDARD FOR ENGLISH

From LETTER DEDICATORY TO THE EARL OF OXFORD

IF it were not for the *Bible* and *Common Prayer Book* in the Vulgar Tongue, we should hardly be able to understand anything that was written among us an hundred years ago; which is certainly true: for those books, being perpetually read in Churches, have proved a kind of standard for language, especially to the common people. And I doubt whether the alterations since introduced have added much to the beauty or strength of the *English* Tongue, though they have taken off a great deal from that *Simplicity* which is one of the greatest perfections in any language. You, my Lord, who are so conversant in the sacred writings, and so great a judge of them in their originals, will agree, that no Translation our Country ever yet produced, has come up to that of the *Old* and *New Testament*: And by the many beautiful passages which I have often had the honour to hear your Lordship cite from thence, I am persuaded that the Translators of the *Bible* were Masters of an *English* style much fitter for that work than any we see in our present writings; which I take to be owing to the *Simplicity* that runs through the whole. Then, as to the greatest part of our *Liturgy*, compiled long before the Translation of the *Bible* now in use, and little altered since, there seem to be in it as great strains of true sublime eloquence as are anywhere to be found in our language; which every man of good Taste will observe in the *Communion Service*, that of *Burial*, and other parts.

¶ GULLIVER CAPTURES THE FLEET OF BLEFUSCU

From A VOYAGE TO LILLIPUT

THE Empire of *Blefuscu* is an Island situated to the North North-East side of *Lilliput*, from whence it is parted only by a Channel of eight hundred Yards wide. I had not yet seen it, and upon this Notice of an intended Invasion, I avoided appearing on that side of the Coast, for fear of being discovered by some of the Enemy's Ships, who had received no Intelligence of me, all Intercourse between the two Empires having been strictly forbidden during the War, upon pain of Death, and an Embargo laid by our Emperor upon all Vessels whatsoever. I communicated to his Majesty a Project I had formed of seizing the Enemy's whole Fleet: which, as our Scouts assured us, lay at Anchor in the Harbour ready to sail with the first fair Wind. I consulted the most experienced Seamen, upon the depth of the Channel, which they had often plumbed, who told me, that in the middle at high Water it was seventy *Glumgluffs* deep, which is about six foot of *European* Measure; and the rest of it fifty *Glumgluffs* at most. I walked towards the North-East Coast over against *Blefuscu*; and lying down behind a Hillock, took out my small Pocket Perspective-Glass, and viewed the Enemy's Fleet at Anchor, consisting of about fifty Men of War, and a great Number of Transports: I then came back to my House, and gave Order (for which I had a Warrant) for a great Quantity of the strongest Cable and Bars of Iron.

The Cable was about as thick as Packthread, and the Bars of the length and size of a Knitting-Needle. I trebled the Cable to make it stronger, and for the same reason I twisted three of the Iron Bars together, binding the Extremities into a Hook. Having thus fixed fifty Hooks to as many Cables, I went back to the North-East Coast, and putting off my Coat, Shoes, and Stockings, walked into the Sea in my Leathern Jerkin, about half an hour before high Water. I waded with what Haste I could, and swam in the middle about thirty Yards till I felt ground; I arrived at the Fleet in less than half an hour. The Enemy was so frighted when they saw me, that they leaped out of their Ships, and swam to shore, where there could not be fewer than thirty thousand Souls. I then took my Tackling, and fastening a Hook to the hole at the Prow of each, I tied all the Cords together at the End. While I was thus employed, the Enemy discharged several thousand Arrows, many of which stuck in my Hands and Face; and besides the excessive smart, gave me much disturbance in my Work. My greatest Apprehension was for my Eyes, which I should have infallibly lost, if I had not suddenly thought of an Expedient. I kept among other little Necessaries a pair of Spectacles in a private Pocket, which, as I observed before, had scaped the Emperor's Searchers. These I took out and fastened as strongly as I could upon my Nose, and thus armed went on boldly with my Work in spite of the Enemy's Arrows, many of which struck against the Glasses of my Spectacles, but without any other Effect, further than a little to discompose them. I had now fastened all the Hooks, and taking the Knot in my Hand, began to pull; but not a Ship would stir, for they were all too fast held by their Anchors, so that the boldest part of my Enterprise remained. I therefore let go the Cord, and leaving the Hooks fixed to the Ships, I resolutely cut with my Knife the Cables that fastened the Anchors, receiving above two hundred Shots in my Face and Hands; then I took up the knotted End of the Cables, to which my Hooks were tied, and with great ease drew fifty of the Enemy's largest Men of War after me.

The *Blefuscudians*, who had not the least Imagination of what I intended, were at first confounded with Astonishment. They had seen me cut the Cables, and thought my Design was only to let the Ships run a-drift, or fall foul on each other: but when they perceived the whole Fleet moving in Order, and saw me pulling at the End, they set up such a scream of Grief and Despair that it is almost impossible to describe or conceive. When I had got out of danger, I stopped awhile to pick out the Arrows that stuck in my Hands and Face; and rubbed on some of the same Ointment that was given me at my first arrival, as I have formerly mentioned. I then took off my Spectacles, and waiting about an Hour, till the Tide was a little fallen, I waded through the middle with my Cargo, and arrived safe at the Royal Port of *Lilliput*.

Joseph Addison

JOSEPH ADDISON (1672–1719) is remembered now only for his essays, but in his day he was a popular poet and dramatist as well as a politician of some note. His poem in celebration of Blenheim—they took notice of such things in those days—won him a post as Under-Secretary of State in succession to Locke; in 1708 he was elected M.P. for Lostwithiel and went as Chief Secretary to Ireland; in 1710 he became M.P. for Malmesbury; and on Anne's death he was secretary to the Regency.

To-day we esteem him not for these things but for the essays—vigorous but urbane, satirical without being bitter, charming but never sloppy—which he contributed to *The Spectator*. The following is typical.

¶ WESTMINSTER ABBEY

From THE SPECTATOR

WHEN I am in a serious Humour, I very often walk by myself in Westminster Abbey; where the Gloominess of the Place, and the Use to which it is applied, with the Solemnity of the Building, and the Condition of the People who lye in it, are apt to fill the Mind with a kind of Melancholy, or rather Thoughtfulness, that is not disagreeable. . . .

For my own part, though I am always serious, I do not know what it is to be melancholy; and can therefore take a View of Nature in her deep and solemn Scenes, with the same Pleasure as in her most gay and delightful ones. By this means I can improve myself with those Objects, which others consider with Terror. When I look upon the Tombs of the Great, every Emotion of Envy dies in me; when I read the Epitaphs of the Beautiful, every inordinate Desire goes out; when I meet with the grief of Parents upon a Tomb-stone, my Heart melts with Compassion; when I see the Tomb of the Parents themselves, I consider the Vanity of grieving for those whom we must quickly follow: When I see Kings lying by those who deposed them, when I consider rival Wits placed Side by Side, or the holy Men that divided the World with their Contests and Disputes, I reflect with Sorrow and Astonishment on the little Competitions, Factions, and Debates of Mankind. When I read the several Dates of the Tombs of some that died Yesterday, and some six hundred Years ago, I consider that great Day when we shall all of us be Contemporaries, and make our Appearance together.

Henry Fielding

HENRY FIELDING (1707–54), one of the earliest and greatest of English novelists expressed in prose not only that balance and sense of the outside world which was common to the eighteenth century, with its freedom from speculative thought and the interior romantic strain; but also a sense of humanity and of common experience which was at that time more rare. It is thought that he learnt something of this as Justice of the Peace for Westminster, where he took a great interest in 'making an effectual provision for the poor'. The voyage to Lisbon, recorded in the Journal from which this extract is taken, was undertaken for the benefit of his health, but it was unsuccessful, and he died there after two months.

¶ LONDON RIVER
From JOURNAL OF A VOYAGE TO LISBON

THE Morning was fair and bright, and we had a Passage thither [to Gravesend], I think, as pleasant as can be conceiv'd; for, take it with all its Advantages, particularly the number of fine Ships you are always sure of seeing by the Way, there is nothing to equal it in all the Rivers of the World. The yards of Deptford and of Woolwich are noble Sights; and give us a just idea of the great Perfection to which we are arrived in building those Floating Castles, and the Figure which we may always make in Europe among the other Maritime Powers. . . .

It is true, perhaps, that there is more of Ostentation than of real Utility, in ships of this vast and unwieldy Burthen, which are rarely capable of acting against an

Enemy; but if the building such contributes to preserve, among other nations, the Notion of the British superiority in Naval Affairs, the expence, though very great, is well incurred, and the Ostentation is laudable and truly political. Indeed, I should be sorry to allow that Holland, France or Spain, possessed a Vessel larger and more beautiful than the largest and most Beautiful of ours; for this Honour I would always administer to the Pride of our Sailors, who should challenge it from all their Neighbours with Truth and Success. And sure I am, that not our honest Tars alone, but every Inhabitant of this Island, may exult in the Comparison, when he considers the King of Great-Britain as a Maritime Prince, in Opposition to any other Prince in Europe; but I am not so certain that the same idea of superiority will result from comparing our Land-forces with those of many other Crowned Heads. In Numbers, they all far exceed us, and in the Goodness and splendor of their troops, many Nations, particularly the Germans and French, and perhaps the Dutch, cast us at a distance. . . .

In our Marine the case is entirely the reverse, and it must be our own Fault if it doth not continue so; for continue so it will, as long as the flourishing State of our Trade shall support it; and this support it can never want, till our Legislature shall cease to give sufficient attention to the Protection of our Trade, and our Magistrates want sufficient Power, Ability, and Honesty to execute the Laws: a circumstance not to be apprehended, as it cannot happen, till our Senates and our Benches shall be filled with the blindest Ignorance, or with the blackest Corruption.

Samuel Johnson

SAMUEL JOHNSON (1709-84) has many claims to greatness. He was our first famous lexicographer. He wrote essays in a style which is a model of strong and elegant English when it is not overladen with latinity. He was one of the most vigorous and brilliant talkers of a period when conversation was an art: the period of his friends Reynolds, Garrick, Beauclerk, and Goldsmith (though poor Oliver was not much of a talker). And, above all, he was a great personality and a man of courage, both physical and moral. All his life he was, in the phrase of Mr. Birrell, 'an old struggler': always against scrofula, and for long against semi-blindness, poverty, and neglect. He could, and did, knock down insolent publishers. And he rejected the belated patronage of Lord Chesterfield in a letter which remains an example of style and independence, of first-rate prose, and sturdy common sense.

I

¶ TO THE RIGHT HONOURABLE THE EARL OF CHESTERFIELD

February 7th, 1755.

MY LORD,

I have been lately informed, by the proprietor of the World, that two papers, in which my Dictionary is recommended to the publick, were written by your Lordship. To be so distinguished, is an honour, which, being very little accustomed to favours from the great, I know not well how to receive, or in what terms to acknowledge.

When, upon some slight encouragement, I first visited your Lordship, I was overpowered, like the rest of mankind, by the enchantment of your address; and could not forbear to wish that I might boast myself *Le vainqueur du vainqueur de la terre;* that I might obtain that regard for which I saw the world contending; but I found my attendance so little encouraged, that neither pride nor modesty would suffer me to continue it. When I had once addressed your Lordship in publick, I had exhausted all the art of pleasing which a retired and uncourtly scholar can possess. I had done all that I could; and no man is well pleased to have his all neglected, be it ever so little.

Seven years, my Lord, have now past, since I waited in your outward rooms, or was repulsed from your door; during which time I have been pushing on my work through difficulties, of which it is useless to complain, and have brought it, at last, to the verge of publication, without one act of assistance, one word of encouragement, or one smile of favour. Such treatment I did not expect, for I never had a Patron before.

The Shepherd in Virgil grew at last acquainted with Love, and found him a native of the rocks.

Is not a Patron, my Lord, one who looks with unconcern on a man struggling for life in the water, and when he has reached ground, encumbers him with help? The notice which you have been pleased to take of my labours, had it been early, had been kind; but it has been delayed until I am indifferent, and cannot enjoy it; till I am solitary, and cannot impart it; till I am known, and do not want it. I hope it is not very cynical asperity not to confess obligations where no benefit has been received, or to be unwilling that the publick should consider me as owing that to a Patron, which Providence has enabled me to do for myself.

Having carried on my work thus far with so little obligation to any favourer of learning, I shall not be disappointed though I should conclude it, if less be possible, with less; for I have been long wakened from that dream of hope, in which I once boasted myself with so much exultation,

>My Lord,
>
>>Your Lordship's most humble,
>>
>>>Most obedient servant,
>>>
>>>>SAM. JOHNSON.

¶ ON HIS DICTIONARY

From the Preface to the ENGLISH DICTIONARY

IN hope of giving longevity to that which its own nature forbids to be immortal, I have devoted this book, the labour of years, to the honour of my country, that we may no longer yield the palm of philology, without a contest, to the nations of the continent.

The chief glory of every people arises from its authours: whether I shall add any thing by my own writings to the reputation of *English* literature, must be left to time: much of my life has been lost under the pressure of disease; much has been trifled away; and much has always been spent in provision for the day that was passing over me; but I shall not think my employment useless or ignoble, if by my assistance foreign nations, and distant ages, gain access to the propagators of knowledge, and understand the teachers of truth; if my labours afford light to the repositories of science, and add celebrity to *Bacon*, to *Hooker*, to *Milton*, and to *Boyle*.

When I am animated by this wish, I look with pleasure on my book, however defective, and deliver it to the world with the spirit of a man that has endeavoured well. That it will immediately become popular I have not promised to myself: a few wild blunders, and risible absurdities, from which no work of such multiplicity was ever free, may for a time furnish folly with laughter, and harden ignorance in contempt; but useful diligence will at last prevail. . . .

In this work, when it shall be found that much is omitted, let it not be forgotten that much likewise is performed; and though no book was ever spared out of tenderness to the authour, and the world is little solicitous to know whence proceeded the faults of that which it condemns; yet it may gratify curiosity to inform it, that the *English Dictionary* was written with little assistance of the learned, and without any patronage of the great; not in the soft obscurities of retirement, or under the shelter of academick bowers, but amidst inconvenience and distraction, in sickness and in sorrow. It may repress the triumph of malignant criticism to observe, that if our language is not here fully displayed, I have only failed in an attempt which no human powers have hitherto completed.

Laurence Sterne

LAURENCE STERNE (1713–68), one of the greatest of English novelists and humorists, was born in Ireland, educated at Jesus College, Cambridge, and destined for the Church. He received the living of Sutton, in Yorkshire, and in holy orders he remained.

He led the life of an ordinary country parson until his forty-seventh year. Then the first portion of *The Life and Opinions of Tristram Shandy* appeared, with such immediate success that Sterne was able to leave for London and bask in his new fame. He was presented with the perpetual curacy of Cotswold and proceeded to lead a literary life. When he was not drinking he wrote. And when his dissipation undermined his health he went to Paris—

where again he was lionized—and travelled on the Continent. The material he picked up thus he used in his *Sentimental Journey*.

¶ THE DEATH OF LE FEVER
From TRISTRAM SHANDY

THE sun looked bright the morning after, to every eye in the village but Le Fever's and his afflicted son's, the hand of death pressed heavy upon his eyelids,—and hardly could the wheel at the cistern turn round its circle,—when my uncle Toby, who had rose up an hour before his wonted time, entered the lieutenant's room and, without preface or apology, sat himself down upon the chair by the bedside, and, independently of all modes and customs, opened the curtain in the manner an old friend and brother-officer would have done it and asked him how he did,—how he had rested in the night,—what was his complaint,—where was his pain,—and what he could do to help him: —and without giving him time to answer any one of the enquiries, went on, and told him of the little plan which he had been concerting with the corporal the night before for him.—

THE CORPORAL AS NURSE

—You shall go home directly, Le Fever, said my uncle Toby, to my house,—and we'll send for a doctor to see what's the matter,—and we'll have an apothecary,—and the corporal shall be your nurse;—and I'll be your servant, Le Fever.

There was a frankness in my uncle Toby,—not the *effect* of familiarity,—but the *cause* of it,—which let you at once into his soul and shewed you the goodness of his nature; to this, there was something in his looks, and voice, and manner, superadded, which eternally beckoned to the unfortunate to come and take shelter under him; so that before my uncle Toby had half-finished the kind offers he was making to the father, had the son insensibly pressed up close to his knees, and had taken hold of the breast of his coat, and was pulling it towards him.—The blood and spirits of Le Fever, which were waxing cold and slow within him, and were retreating to their last citadel, the heart—rallied back,—the film forsook his eyes for a moment,—he looked up wishfully in my uncle Toby's face,—then cast a look upon his boy,—and that *ligament*, fine as it was,—was never broken.

Oliver Goldsmith

OLIVER GOLDSMITH (1728–74) belonged to the Johnson circle and was several times befriended by the great man himself. He is best known by his novel *The Vicar of Wakefield* and his plays. But the generally neglected essays have a high place in the courteous and easy prose of his century, a prose which invited attention and promised persuasion or conviction. *The Citizen of the World* is supposed to be a series of letters from a Chinaman in England to his friend at Pekin, and provides an admirable example of the criticism which the eighteenth century passed upon its own customs and fashions.

¶ A PARTY AT VAUXHALL
From THE CITIZEN OF THE WORLD

THE People of *London* are as fond of walking, as our friends at *Pekin* of riding; one of the principal entertainments of the citizens here in summer, is to repair about nightfall to a garden not far from town, where they walk about, shew their best cloaths and best faces, and listen to a concert provided for the occasion.

I accepted an invitation a few evenings ago from my old friend, the man in black, to be one of a party that was to sup there, and at the appointed hour waited upon him at his lodgings. There I found the company assembled and expecting my arrival. Our party consisted of my friend in superlative finery, his stockings rolled, a black velvet waistcoat, which was formerly new, and his grey wig combed down in imitation of hair. A pawn-broker's widow, of whom, by the bye, my friend was a professed admirer, dressed out in green damask, with three gold rings on every finger. Mr. *Tibbs*, the second-rate beau, I have formerly described, together with his lady, in flimsy silk, dirty gauze instead of linnen, and an hat as big as an umbrella. . . .

The illuminations began before we arrived, and I must confess, that upon entring the gardens, I found every sense overpaid with more than expected pleasure; the lights every where glimmering through the scarcely moving trees; the full-bodied concert bursting on the stillness of the night, the natural concert of the birds in the more retired part of the grove, vying with that which was formed by art; the company gayly dressed, looking satisfaction, and the tables spread with various delicacies, all conspired to fill my imagination with the visionary happiness of the *Arabian* lawgiver, and lifted me into an extasy of admiration. Head of *Confucius*, cried I to my friend, this is fine! this unites rural beauty with courtly magnificence; if we except the virgins of immortality that hang on every tree, and may be plucked at every desire, I don't see how this falls short of *Mahomet's Paradise!* As for virgins, cries my friend, it is true they are a fruit that don't much abound in our gardens here; but if ladies as plenty as apples in autumn, and as complying as any *hoüry* of them all, can content you, I fancy we have no need to go to heaven for Paradise.

I was going to second his remarks, when we were called to a consultation by Mr. *Tibbs* and the rest of the company, to know in what manner we were to lay out the evening to the greatest advantage. Mrs. *Tibbs* was for keeping the genteel walk of the garden, where she observed there was always the very best company; the widow, on the contrary, who came but once a season, was for securing a good standing-place to see the water-works, which she assured us would begin in less than an hour at farthest; a dispute therefore began, and as it was managed between two of very opposite characters, it threatened to grow more bitter at every reply. Mrs. *Tibbs* wondered how people could pretend to know the polite world, who had received all their rudiments of breeding behind a compter; to which the other replied, that tho' some people sat behind compters, yet they could sit at the head of their own tables too, and carve three good dishes of hot meat whenever they thought proper, which was more than some people could say for themselves, that hardly knew a rabbet and onions from a green goose and gooseberries.

It is hard to say where this might have ended, had not the husband, who probably knew the impetuosity of his wife's disposition, proposed to end the dispute by adjourning to a box, and try if there was any thing to be had for supper that was supportable. . . .

Mr. *Tibbs* now willing to prove that his wife's pretensions to music were just, entreated her to favour the company with a song; but to this she gave a positive denial, for you know very well, my dear, says she, that I am not in voice to day, and when one's voice is not equal to one's judgment, what signifies singing; besides, as there is no accompanyment, it would be but spoiling music. All these excuses however were overruled by the rest of the company, who though one would think they already had music enough, joined in the intreaty. But particularly the widow, now willing to convince the company of her breeding, pressed so warmly, that she seemed determined to take no refusal. At last, then, the lady complied, and after humming for some minutes, began with such a voice and such affectation, as, I could perceive, gave but little satisfaction to any except her husband. He sat with rapture in his eye, and beat time with his hand on the table.

You must observe, my friend, that it is the custom of this country, when a lady or gentleman happens to sing, for the company to sit as mute and as motionless as statues. Every feature, every limb must seem to correspond in fixed attention, and while the song continues, they are to remain in a state of universal petrefaction. In this mortifying situation we had continued for some time, listening to the song, and looking with tranquillity, when the master of the box came to inform us that the water-works were going to begin. At this information, I could instantly perceive the widow bounce from her seat; but correcting herself, she sat down again, repressed by motives of good breeding. Mrs. *Tibbs*, who had seen the water-works an hundred times, resolved not to be interrupted, continued her song without any share of mercy, nor had the smallest pity on our impatience. The widow's face, I own, gave me high entertainment; in it I could plainly read the struggle she felt between good breeding and curiosity; she talked of the water-works the whole evening before, and seemed to have come merely in order to see them; but then she could not bounce out in the very middle of a song, for that would be forfeiting all pretensions to high-life, or high-lived company ever after: Mrs. *Tibbs*, therefore, kept on singing, and we continued to listen, till at last, when the song was just concluded, the waiter came to inform us that the water-works were over!

The water-works over, cried the widow! the water-works over already, that's impossible, they can't be over so soon! It is not my business, replied the fellow, to contradict your ladyship, I'll run again and see; he went, and soon returned with a confirmation of the dismal tidings. No ceremony could now bind my friend's disappointed mistress, she testified her displeasure in the openest manner; in short, she now began to find fault in turn, and at last, insisted upon going home, just at the time that Mr. and Mrs. *Tibbs* assured the company, that the polite hours were going to begin, and that the ladies would instantaneously be entertained with the horns.

Edmund Burke

EDMUND BURKE (1729-97), an Irishman by birth, practised at the English bar and sat most of his life in the English House of Commons. Though he never held any higher office than that of Paymaster-General, he was the philosophical brain behind the Whig party in the first half of George III's reign. He transformed the basis of the party from a system of family alliances and vested interests to a reasoned political creed. As a political pamphleteer he stood in the first rank, and he is the greatest orator in the history of Parliament.

¶ MARIE ANTOINETTE
From REFLECTIONS ON THE REVOLUTION IN FRANCE

IT is now sixteen or seventeen years since I saw the Queen of France, then the Dauphiness, at Versailles; and surely never lighted on this orb, which she hardly seemed to touch, a more delightful vision. I saw her just above the horizon, decorating and cheering the elevated sphere she just began to move in; glittering like the morning star, full of life, and splendor, and joy. Oh! what a revolution! and what an heart must I have, to contemplate without emotion that elevation and that fall! Little did I dream when she added titles of veneration to those of enthusiastic, distant, respectful love, that she should ever be obliged to carry the sharp antidote against disgrace concealed in that bosom; little did I dream that I should have lived to see such disasters fallen upon her in a nation of gallant men, in a nation of men of honour and of cavaliers. I thought ten thousand swords must have leaped from their scabbards to avenge even a look that threatened her with insult.— But the age of chivalry is gone. That of sophisters, œconomists, and calculators, has succeeded; and the glory of Europe is extinguished for ever. Never, never more, shall we behold that generous loyalty to rank and sex, that proud submission, that dignified obedience, that subordination of the heart, which kept alive, even in servitude itself, the spirit of an exalted freedom. The unbought grace of life, the cheap defence of nations, the nurse of manly sentiment and heroic enterprize, is gone! It is gone, that sensibility of principle, that chastity of honour, which felt a stain like a wound, which inspired courage whilst it mitigated ferocity, which ennobled whatever it touched, and under which vice itself lost half its evil, by losing all its grossness.

Edward Gibbon

EDWARD GIBBON (1737-94) remains, with the possible exception of Macaulay, the most celebrated and popular of English historians. The son of a London merchant, he was sent to Westminster School and then educated privately—mainly through his own voracious reading. Arriving at Magdalen College, Oxford, 'with a stock of information which might have puzzled a doctor and a degree of ignorance of which a schoolboy might be ashamed,' he stayed only fourteen unsatisfactory months and was then placed under a tutor at Lausanne. From this time onwards he devoted himself to literature. His *Autobiography* is one of the first in the language; but he is famous, of course, chiefly for his *Decline and Fall of the Roman Empire*, one of the most majestic of all literary landmarks in the grand manner.

How he began and ended this work is described below.

¶ GIBBON ON HIS LIFE WORK
From MEMOIRS OF MY LIFE AND WRITINGS

I

IT was at Rome, on the 15th October, 1764, as I sat musing amidst the ruins of the Capitol, while the barefooted fryars were singing vespers in the Temple of Jupiter, that the idea of writing the decline and fall of the city first started to my mind. But my original plan was circumscribed to the decay of the city rather than of the empire; and, though my reading and reflections began to point towards that object, some years elapsed, and several avocations intervened, before I was seriously engaged in the execution of that laborious work.

II

I have presumed to mark the moment of conception; I shall now commemorate the hour of my final deliverance. It was on the day, or rather night, of the 27th June, 1787, between the hours of eleven and twelve, that I wrote the last line of the last page, in a summer-house in my garden. After laying down my pen I took several turns in a berceau, or covered walk of acacias, which commands a prospect of the country, the lake, and the mountains. The air was temperate, the sky was serene, the silver orb of the moon was reflected from the waters, and all nature was silent. I will not dissemble the first emotions of joy on the recovery of my freedom and, perhaps, the establishment of my fame. But my pride was soon humbled, and a sober melancholy was spread over my mind, by the idea that I had taken an everlasting leave of an old and agreeable companion, and that whatsoever might be the future date of my History, the life of the historian must be short and precarious.

William Wordsworth

WILLIAM WORDSWORTH (1770–1850) is of course one of England's greatest poets. The story of his early partnership with Coleridge has often been told. Coleridge was to make the fantastic credible, and in doing so did more than any one else to found the Romantic school in England. Wordsworth's part was to reveal the poetry and romance of common simple things.

There were times when he succeeded as magnificently as did Coleridge. There were other times—I hope no child knows them—when this man of genius fell into sheer bathos.

'Every great poet is a teacher,' he declared, and the didactic character of much of his verse is reflected also in the preachiness of his prose. But in prose, as in poetry, he often contrived to speak with the accents of authentic greatness.

¶ THE POET
From the Preface to LYRICAL BALLADS

TO this knowledge which all men carry about with them, and to these sympathies in which, without any other discipline than that of our daily life, we are fitted to take delight, the Poet principally directs his attention. He considers man and nature as essentially adapted to each other, and the mind of man as naturally the mirror of the fairest and most interesting properties of nature. And thus the Poet, prompted by this feeling of pleasure, which accompanies him through the whole course of his studies, converses with general nature, with affections akin to those, which, through labour and length of time, the Man of Science has raised up in himself, by conversing with those particular parts of nature which are the objects of his studies.

The knowledge both of the Poet and the Man of Science is pleasure; but the knowledge of the one cleaves to us as a necessary part of our existence, our natural and unalienable inheritance; the other is a personal and individual acquisition, slow to come to us and by no habitual and direct sympathy connecting us with our fellow-beings. The Man of Science seeks truth as a remote and unknown benefactor; he cherishes and loves it in his solitude: the Poet, singing a song in which all human beings join with him, rejoices in the presence of truth as our visible friend and hourly companion. Poetry is the breath and finer spirit of all knowledge; it is the impassioned expression which is in the countenance of all Science.

Emphatically may it be said of the Poet, as Shakespeare hath said of man, 'that he looks before and after'. He is the rock of defence for human nature; an upholder and preserver, carrying everywhere with him relationship and love. In spite of difference of soil and climate, of language and manners, of laws and customs: in spite of things silently gone out of mind, and things violently destroyed; the Poet binds together by passion and knowledge the vast empire of human society, as it is spread over the whole earth, and over all time.

Sir Walter Scott

SIR WALTER SCOTT (1771–1832), one of the most romantic minds of a romantic age, achieved in the Waverley Novels two separate triumphs, of which the two following extracts are examples. The second—and less important—is his romantic melodrama; he likes —and we like in him—titles, colour, crises, and the resounding phrase, and incidents in which he can use them are frequent. But he had also a profound sense of the dignity and solemn rights of every individual—the beggar, the exile, the prisoner, the gipsy. He excels therefore when he has an opportunity of allowing that high humanity to express itself in noble words, and such is the first extract given here.

¶ THE LAIRD EVICTS THE GIPSIES
From GUY MANNERING

CERTAIN qualms of feeling had deterred Ellangowan from attending in person to see his tenants expelled. He left the executive part of the business to the officers of the law. . . .

Mr. Bertram himself chose that day to make a visit to a friend at some distance. But it so happened, notwithstanding his precautions, that he could not avoid meeting his late tenants during their retreat from his property.

It was in a hollow way, near the top of a steep ascent, upon the verge of the Ellangowan estate, that Mr. Bertram met the gipsy procession. Four or five men formed the advanced guard, wrapped in long loose greatcoats that hid their tall slender figures, as the large slouched hats, drawn over their brows, concealed their wild features, dark eyes, and swarthy faces. Two of them carried long fowling-pieces, one wore a broadsword without a sheath, and all had the Highland dirk, though they did not wear that weapon openly or ostentatiously. Behind them followed the train of laden asses, and small carts, or *tumblers* as they were called in that country, on which were laid the decrepit and the helpless, the aged and infant part of the exiled community. The women in their red cloaks and straw hats, the elder children with bare heads and bare feet, and almost naked bodies, had the immediate care of the little caravan. The road was narrow, running between two broken banks of sand. . . .

When the Laird had pressed on with difficulty among a crowd of familiar faces, which had on all former occasions marked his approach with the reverence due to that of a superior being, but in which he now only read hatred and contempt, and had got clear of the throng, he could not help turning his horse, and looking back to mark the progress of their march. . . .

The van had already reached a small and stunted thicket, which was at the bottom of the hill, and which gradually hid the line of march until the last stragglers disappeared.

His sensations were bitter enough. The race, it is true, which he had thus summarily dismissed from their ancient place of refuge, was idle and vicious; but had he endeavoured to render them otherwise? They were not more irregular characters now, than they had been while they were admitted to consider themselves as a sort of subordinate dependants of his family; and ought the mere circumstance of his becoming a magistrate to have made at once such a change in his conduct towards them? Some means of reformation ought at least to have been tried, before sending seven families at once upon the wide world, and depriving them of a degree of countenance which withheld them at least from atrocious guilt. There was also a natural yearning of heart on parting with so many known and familiar faces; and to this feeling Godfrey Bertram was peculiarly accessible, from the limited qualities of his mind, which sought its principal amusements among the petty objects around him. As he was about to turn his horse's head to pursue his journey, Meg Merrilies, who had lagged behind the troop, unexpectedly presented herself.

She was standing upon one of those high precipitous banks, which, as we before noticed, overhung the road; so that she was placed considerably higher than Ellangowan, even though he was on horseback; and her tall figure, relieved against the clear blue sky, seemed almost of supernatural stature. We have noticed that there was in her general attire, or rather in her mode of adjusting it, somewhat of a foreign costume, artfully adopted perhaps for the purpose of adding to the effect of her spells and predictions, or perhaps from some traditional notions respecting the dress of her ancestors. On this occasion, she had a large piece of red cotton cloth rolled about her head in the form of a turban, from beneath which her dark eyes flashed with uncommon lustre. Her long and tangled black hair fell in elf-locks from the folds of this singular head-gear. Her attitude was that of a sibyl in frenzy, and she stretched out in her right hand a sapling bough, which seemed just pulled.

'I'll be d——d,' said the groom, 'if she has not been cutting the young ashes in the Dukit park!'—The Laird made no answer, but continued to look at the figure which was thus perched above his path.

'Ride your ways,' said the gipsy, 'ride your ways,

Laird of Ellangowan—ride your ways, Godfrey Bertram!—This day have ye quenched seven smoking hearths—see if the fire in your ain parlour burn the blither for that. Ye have riven the thack off seven cottar houses—look if your ain roof-tree stand the faster.—Ye may stable your stirks in the shealings at Derncleugh—see that the hare does not couch on the hearthstane at Ellangowan.—Ride your ways, Godfrey Bertram—what do ye glower after our folk for?—There's thirty hearts there, that wad hae wanted bread ere ye had wanted sunkets, and spent their life-blood ere ye had scratched your finger. Yes—there's thirty yonder, from the auld wife of an hundred to the babe that was born last week, that ye have turned out o' their bits o' bields, to sleep with the tod and the blackcock in the muirs!—Ride your ways, Ellangowan.—Our bairns are hinging at our weary backs—look that your braw cradle at hame be the fairer spread up: not that I'm wishing ill to little Harry, or to the babe that's yet to be born—God forbid—and make them kind to the poor, and better folk than their father!—And now, ride e'en your ways; for these are the last words ye'll ever hear Meg Merrilies speak, and this is the last reise that I'll ever cut in the bonny woods of Ellangowan.'

So saying, she broke the sapling she held in her hand, and flung it into the road. Margaret of Anjou, bestowing on her triumphant foes her keen-edged malediction, could not have turned from them with a gesture more proudly contemptuous. The Laird was clearing his voice to speak, and thrusting his hand in his pocket to find a half-crown; the gipsy waited neither for his reply nor his donation, but strode down the hill to overtake the caravan.

Ellangowan rode pensively home; and it was remarkable that he did not mention this interview to any of his family. The groom was not so reserved; he told the story at great length to a full audience in the kitchen, and concluded by swearing, that 'if ever the devil spoke by the mouth of a woman, he had spoken by that of Meg Merrilies that blessed day'.

¶ THE BANNER OF ENGLAND
From THE TALISMAN

THE king was soon at the foot of St. George's Mount, the sides as well as platform of which were now surrounded and crowded, partly by those belonging to the Duke of Austria's retinue, who were celebrating, with shouts of jubilee, the act which they considered as an assertion of national honour; partly by bystanders of different nations, whom dislike to the English, or mere curiosity, had assembled together, to witness the end of these extraordinary proceedings. Through this disorderly troop Richard burst his way, like a goodly ship under full sail, which cleaves her forcible passage through the rolling billows, and heeds not that they unite after her passage and roar upon her stern. . . .

'Who has dared,' he said, laying his hands upon the Austrian standard, and speaking in a voice like the sound which precedes an earthquake; 'who has dared to place this paltry rag beside the banner of England?'

The archduke wanted not personal courage, and it was impossible he could hear this question without reply. Yet, so much was he troubled and surprised by the unexpected arrival of Richard, and affected by the general awe inspired by his ardent and unyielding character, that the demand was twice repeated, in a tone which seemed to challenge heaven and earth, ere the archduke replied with such firmness as he could command, 'It was I, Leopold of Austria.'

'Then shall Leopold of Austria,' replied Richard, 'presently see the rate at which his banner and his pretensions are held by Richard of England.'

So saying, he pulled up the standard-spear, splintered it to pieces, threw the banner itself on the ground, and placed his foot upon it.

'Thus,' said he, 'I trample on the banner of Austria—Is there a knight among your Teutonic chivalry, dare impeach my deed?'

There was a momentary silence; but there are no braver men than the Germans.

'I,' and 'I,' and 'I,' was heard from several knights of the duke's followers; and he himself added his voice to those which accepted the King of England's defiance.

'Why do we dally thus?' said the Earl Wallenrode, a gigantic warrior from the frontiers of Hungary: 'Brethren, and noble gentlemen, this man's foot is on the honour of your country—Let us rescue it from violation, and down with the pride of England!'

So saying, he drew his sword, and struck at the king a blow which might have proved fatal, had not the Scot intercepted and caught it upon his shield.

'I have sworn,' said King Richard—and his voice was heard above all the tumult, which now waxed wild and loud—'never to strike one whose shoulder bears the cross; therefore live, Wallenrode—but live to remember Richard of England.'

As he spoke, he grasped the tall Hungarian round the waist, and, unmatched in wrestling as in other military exercises, hurled him backwards with such violence that the mass flew as if discharged from a military engine, not only through the ring of spectators who witnessed the extraordinary scene, but over the edge of the mount itself, down the steep side of which Wallenrode rolled headlong, until, pitching at length upon his shoulder, he dislocated the bone, and lay like one dead.

Charles Lamb

IT is difficult to write of Charles Lamb (1775–1834) without overworking two words—'whimsical' and 'charm'. For his essays, published as by '*Elia*,' are distinguished to an extraordinary degree by the qualities which those words denote. His humour is as individual as his style. He is at once recklessly imaginative and the embodiment of common sense, intensely personal without being egotistic, wistful but never sloppy. Entrusted with the care of his sister Mary, who was at times mad, and in one frenzy stabbed to death her mother, Charles Lamb devoted his life to her and never married. But for a long while he was hopelessly in love, and his wistful dreams of what might have been are revealed in 'Dream Children', an extract from *Elia*.

¶ DREAM CHILDREN
From ESSAYS OF ELIA

HERE the children fell a-crying, and asked if their little mourning which they had on was not for Uncle John, and they looked up and prayed me not to go on about their uncle, but to tell them some stories about their pretty dead mother. Then I told how for seven long years, in hope sometimes, sometimes in despair, yet persisting ever, I courted the fair Alice W——n; and, as much as children could understand, I explained to them what coyness, and difficulty, and denial meant in maidens—when suddenly, turning to Alice, the soul of the first Alice looked out at her eyes with such a reality of re-presentment, that I became in doubt which of them stood there before me, or whose that bright hair was; and while I stood gazing, both the children gradually grew fainter to my view, receding, and still receding till nothing at last but two mournful features were seen in the uttermost distance, which, without speech, strangely impressed upon me the effects of speech: 'We are not of Alice, nor of thee, nor are we children at all. The children of Alice call Bartrum father. We are nothing; less than nothing, and dreams. We are only what might have been, and must wait upon the tedious shores of Lethe millions of ages before we have existence, and a name'—and immediately awaking, I found myself quietly seated in my bachelor arm-chair, where I had fallen asleep.

Walter Savage Landor

WALTER SAVAGE LANDOR (1775–1864) was one of the most prolific writers of the nineteenth century. When he raised a regiment at his own expense and led it against the French in the Peninsular War, it might have seemed that he was destined to the life of a man of action. But that enterprise came to little and he returned to England to continue his career as a writer of prose and verse in English, Latin, and Italian. He continued to write to the very end of his long life. His verse though lofty and magnificent in tone, and though extravagantly praised by Swinburne, is now less read than it should be. It is, like his prose, capable of extreme nobility and extreme tenderness.

¶ AESOP AND RHODOPE
From IMAGINARY CONVERSATIONS

Rhodope: Let me pause and consider a little, if you please. I begin to suspect that, as gods formerly did, you have been turning men into beasts, and beasts into men. But, Aesop, you should never say the thing that is untrue.

Aesop: We say and do and look no other all our lives.

Rhodope: Do we never know better?

Aesop: Yes; when we cease to please, and to wish it; when death is settling the features, and the cerements are ready to render them unchangeable.

Rhodope: Alas! Alas!

Aesop: Breathe, Rhodope! breathe again those painless sighs: they belong to thy vernal season. May thy summer of life be calm: thy autumn calmer, and thy winter never come!

Rhodope: I must die then earlier.

Aesop: Laodameia died; Helen died; Leda, the beloved of Jupiter, went before. It is better to repose in the earth betimes than to sit up late; better, than to cling pertinaciously to what we feel crumbling under us, and to protract an inevitable fall. We may enjoy the present, while we are insensible of infirmity and decay; but the present, like a note in music, is nothing but as it appertains to what is past and what is to come. There are no fields of amaranth on this side of the grave; there are no voices, O Rhodope, that are not soon mute, however tuneful; there is no name, with whatever emphasis of passionate love repeated, of which the echo is not faint at last.

Rhodope: O Aesop; let me rest my head on yours: it throbs and pains me.

Aesop: What are these ideas to thee?

Rhodope: Sad, sorrowful.

Aesop: Harrows that break the soil, preparing it for wisdom. Many flowers must perish ere a grain of corn be ripened. And now remove thy head; the cheek is cool enough after its little shower of tears.

William Hazlitt

WILLIAM HAZLITT (1778–1830) is one of the great English critics—in such books as the *Characters of Shakespeare's Plays*, the *English Poets*, *English Comic Writers*, and so on. But in Hazlitt this genius was part of a general interest in everything, and it is his capacity for loving and hating, his 'enjoyment' of it, which makes his criticism important, his essays vital, and even his controversy still exciting. He was acquainted with Coleridge and Wordsworth and Lamb and the rest of their friends; he quarrelled with most of them, saw his political dreams destroyed, was financially harassed, troubled in many ways, and at the end of all said 'Well, I have had a happy life'.

¶ JOHN CAVANAGH
From TABLE-TALK

DIED at his house in Burbage Street, St. Giles's, John Cavanagh, the famous hand fives-player. When a person dies who does any one thing better than any one else in the world, which so many others are trying to do well, it leaves a gap in society. It is not likely that any one will now see the game of fives played in its perfection for many years to come—for Cavanagh is dead, and has not left his peer behind him.

It may be said that there are things of more importance than striking a ball against a wall—there are things, indeed, that make more noise and do as little good, such as making war and peace, making speeches and answering them, making verses and blotting them, making money and throwing it away. But the game of fives is what no one despises who has ever played at it. It is the finest exercise for the body, and the best relaxation for the mind. The Roman poet said that 'Care mounted behind the horseman and stuck to his skirts'. But this remark would not have applied to the fives-player. He who takes to playing at fives is twice young.

He feels neither the past nor future 'in the instant'. Debts, taxes, 'domestic treason, foreign levy, nothing can touch him further'. He has no other wish, no other thought from the moment the game begins, but that of striking the ball, of placing it, of *making* it! This Cavanagh was sure to do. Whenever he touched the ball there was an end of the chase. His eye was certain, his hand fatal, his presence of mind complete. He could do what he pleased, and he always knew exactly what to do. He saw the whole game, and played it; took instant advantage of his adversary's weakness, and recovered balls, as if by a miracle and from sudden thought, that every one gave for lost. He had equal power and skill, quickness, and judgement. He could either outwit his antagonist by finesse, or beat him by main strength. Sometimes, when he seemed preparing to send the ball with the full swing of his arm, he would by a slight turn of his wrist drop it within an inch of the line. In general, the ball came from his hand, as if from a racket, in a straight, horizontal line; so that it was in vain to attempt to overtake or stop it. As it was said of a great orator that he never was at a loss for a word, and for the properest word, so Cavanagh always could tell the degree of force necessary to be given to a ball, and the precise direction in which it should be sent. He did his work with the greatest ease; never took more pains than was necessary; and, while others were fagging themselves to death, was as cool and collected as if he had just entered the court. His style of play was as remarkable as his power of execution. He had no affectation, no trifling. He did not throw away the game to show off an attitude or try an experiment. He was a fine, sensible, manly player, who did what he could, but that was more than any one else could even affect to do. His blows were not undecided and ineffectual—lumbering like Mr. Wordsworth's epic poetry, nor wavering like Mr. Coleridge's lyric prose, nor short of the mark like Mr. Brougham's speeches, nor wide of it like Mr. Canning's wit, nor foul like the *Quarterly*, nor *let* balls like the *Edinburgh Review*. Cobbett and Junius together would have made a Cavanagh. He was the best *up-hill* player in the world; even when his adversary was fourteen he would play on the same or better, and as he never flung away the game through carelessness and conceit, he never gave it up through laziness or want of heart. The only peculiarity of his play was that he never *volleyed*, but let the balls hop; but if they rose an inch from the ground he never missed having them. There was not only nobody equal, but nobody second to him. It is supposed that he could give any other player half the game, or beat them with his left hand....

Cavanagh was an Irishman by birth, and a housepainter by profession. He had once laid aside his working-dress, and walked up, in his smartest clothes, to the Rosemary Branch to have an afternoon's pleasure. A person accosted him, and asked him if he would have a game. So they agreed to play for half a crown a game and a bottle of cider. The first game began—it was seven, eight, ten, thirteen, fourteen, all. Cavanagh won it. The next was the same. They played on, and each game was hardly contested. 'There,' said the unconscious fives-player, 'there was a stroke that Cavanagh could not take: I never played better in my life, and yet I can't win a game. I don't know how it is!' However, they played on, Cavanagh winning every game, and the bystanders drinking the cider and laughing all the time. In the twelfth game, when Cavanagh was only four, and the stranger thirteen, a person came in and said, 'What! are you here, Cavanagh?' The words were no sooner pronounced than the astonished player let the ball drop from his hand, and saying, 'What! have I been breaking my heart all this time to beat Cavanagh?' refused to make another effort. 'And yet, I give you my word,' said Cavanagh, telling the story with some triumph, 'I played all the while with my clenched fist.' . . .

He could not have shown himself in any ground in England but he would have been immediately surrounded with inquisitive gazers, trying to find out in what part of his frame his unrivalled skill lay, as politicians wonder to see the balance of Europe suspended in Lord Castlereagh's face, and admire the trophies of the British Navy lurking under Mr. Croker's hanging brow. Now Cavanagh was as good-looking a man as the noble Lord, and much better looking than the Right Hon. Secretary. He had a clear, open countenance, and did not look sideways or down, like Mr. Murray the bookseller. He was a young fellow of sense, humour, and courage. He once had a quarrel with a waterman at Hungerford Stairs, and, they say, served him out in great style. In a word, there are hundreds at this day who cannot mention his name without admiration, as the best fives-player that perhaps ever lived (the greatest excellence of which they have any notion); and the noisy shout of the ring happily stood him in stead of the unheard voice of posterity! . . . We have paid this willing tribute to his memory.

> Let no rude hand deface it
> And his forlorn '*Hic Jacet*'.

Thomas De Quincey

THOMAS DE QUINCEY (1785–1859), after leaving Worcester College, Oxford, became one of the earliest disciples of the Lake School of English poetry. His own works, however, were nearly all in prose, and he became the master of an elaborate and fantastic style, recounting dreams and nightmares, such as might have been expected of the opium-eater he was. Some of his sentences, piling clause on clause to dizzy heights of ecstasy, remind the reader of the wilder flights of Gothic architecture. But if he dealt with nightmares he dealt with them carefully: his style has dizzy heights but preserves always the interior balance.

¶ OUR LADIES OF SORROW
From SUSPIRIA DE PROFUNDIS

'THESE are the Sorrows; and they are three in number, as the Graces are three, who dress man's life with beauty; the Parcae are three, who weave the dark arras of man's life in their mysterious loom always with colours sad in part, sometimes angry with tragic crimson and black; the Furies are three, who visit with retributions called from the other side of the grave offences that walk upon this; and once even the Muses were but three, who fit the harp, the trumpet, or the lute, to the great burdens of man's impassioned creations. These are the Sorrows, all three of whom I know.' The last words I say *now*; but in Oxford I said—'One of whom I know, and the others too surely I *shall* know.' For already, in my fervent youth, I saw (dimly relieved upon the dim background of my dreams) the imperfect lineaments of the awful sisters.

The eldest of the three is named Mater Lachrymarum, Our Lady of Tears. She it is that night and day raves and moans, calling for vanished faces. She stood in Rama, when a voice was heard of lamentation—Rachel weeping for her children, and refusing to be comforted. She it was that stood in Bethlehem on the night when Herod's sword swept its nurseries of Innocents and the little feet were stiffened for ever, which heard at times as they tottered along floors overhead, woke pulses of love in household hearts that were not unmarked in heaven.

Her eyes are sweet and subtle, wild and sleepy by turns; oftentimes rising to the clouds; oftentimes challenging the heavens. She wears a diadem round her head. And I knew by childish memories that she could go abroad upon the winds, when she heard the sobbing of litanies or the thundering of organs, and when she beheld the mustering of summer clouds. This sister, the elder, it is that carries keys more than papal at her girdle, which open every cottage and every palace. . .

By the power of her keys it is that Our Lady of Tears glides a ghostly intruder into the chambers of sleepless men, sleepless women, sleepless children. . . .

Every captive in every dungeon;—all that are betrayed, and all that are rejected; outcasts by traditionary law, and children of hereditary disgrace—all these walk with Our Lady of Sighs. She also carries a key; but she needs it little. For her kingdom is chiefly amongst the tents of Shem, and the household vagrant of every clime. Yet in the very highest ranks of man she finds chapels of her own; and even in glorious England there are some that, to the world, carry their heads as proudly as the reindeer, who yet secretly have received her mark upon their foreheads.

But the third sister, who is also the youngest—Hush! whisper, whilst we talk of *her*! Her kingdom is not large, or else no flesh should live; but within that kingdom all power is hers. Her head, turreted like that of Cybele, rises almost beyond the reach of sight. She droops not; and her eyes rising so high, *might* be hidden by distance. But, being what they are, they cannot be hidden; through the treble veil of crape which she wears, the fierce light of a blazing misery, that rests not for matins or for vespers—for noon of day or noon of night—for ebbing or flowing of tide—may be read from the very ground. She is the defier of God. She also is the mother of lunacies, and the suggestress of suicides. Deep lie the roots of her power; but narrow is the nation that she rules. For she can approach only those in whom a profound nature has been upheaved by central convulsions; in whom the heart trembles and the brain rocks under conspiracies of tempest from without and tempest from within. Madonna moves with uncertain steps, fast or slow, but still with tragic grace. Our Lady of Sighs creeps timidly and stealthily. But this youngest sister moves with incalculable motions, bounding, and with a tiger's leaps. She carries no key; for, though coming rarely among men, she storms all doors at which she is permitted to enter at all. And her name is Mater Tenebrarum—Our Lady of Darkness.

These were the Semnai Theai, or Sublime Goddesses —these were the Eumenides, or Gracious Ladies (so called by antiquity in shuddering propitiation)—of my Oxford dreams.

Sir William Napier

SIR WILLIAM NAPIER (1785–1860), a member of one of our most illustrious military families, entered the British Army at the age of 15 and was only 28 when he commanded a regiment which formed part of the Light Brigade. He was present at the siege of Copenhagen in 1807 and the Battle of Corunna (where Sir John Moore was killed) in 1809, served through the Peninsular War with great distinction, was knighted in 1848 and promoted to general in 1859, and died in the following year.

Gallant soldier though he was, his principal claim to remembrance is his *History of the Peninsular War*; its style has 'the strength and majesty' of which he wrote.

¶ ALBUERA

From THE HISTORY OF THE PENINSULAR WAR

AT this time six guns were in the enemy's possession, the whole of Werlé's reserves were coming forward to reinforce the front column of the French, the remnant of Houghton's brigade could no longer maintain its ground, the field was heaped with carcasses, the lancers were riding furiously about the captured artillery on the upper parts of the hill, and behind all, Hamilton's Portuguese and Alten's Germans, now withdrawing from the bridge, seemed to be in full retreat. Soon, however, Cole's fusiliers, flanked by a battalion of the Lusitanian legion under Colonel Hawkshawe, mounted the hill, drove off the lancers, recovered five of the captured guns and one colour....

Such a gallant line, issuing from the midst of the smoke and rapidly separating itself from the confused and broken multitude, startled the enemy's masses, which were increasing and pressing onwards as to an assured victory; they wavered, hesitated, and then vomiting forth a storm of fire, hastily endeavoured to enlarge their front, while a fearful discharge of grape from all their artillery whistled through the British ranks. Myers was killed, Cole and the three colonels, Ellis, Blakeney, and Hawkshawe, fell wounded, and the fusilier battalions, struck by the iron tempest, reeled and staggered like sinking ships; but suddenly and sternly recovering they closed on their terrible enemies, and then was seen with what a strength and majesty the British soldier fights. In vain did Soult with voice and gesture animate his Frenchmen, in vain did the hardiest veterans break from the crowded columns and sacrifice their lives to gain time for the mass to open out on such a fair field; in vain did the mass itself bear up, and, fiercely striving, fire indiscriminately upon friends and foes, while the horsemen hovering on the flank threatened to charge the advancing line.

Nothing could stop that astonishing infantry. No sudden burst of undisciplined valour, no nervous enthusiasm weakened the stability of their order, their flashing eyes were bent on the dark columns in their front, their measured tread shook the ground, their dreadful volleys swept away the head of every formation, their deafening shouts overpowered the dissonant cries that broke from all parts of the tumultuous crowd, as slowly and with a horrid carnage it was pushed by the incessant vigour of the attack to the farthest edge of the hill.

Thomas Carlyle

THOMAS CARLYLE (1795–1881) was the son of a small Scottish farmer, but came to London early in life and, after a hard struggle, established himself in the profession of letters. He wrote in many forms—history, biography, philosophy, and belles lettres, but in all his writings he is pre-eminently a satirist and a social reformer. In his great works on the French Revolution, on Frederick the Great, and on Cromwell, he used the lessons of the past to denounce the evils of his own day. The basis of his political philosophy was twofold—to insist on an active policy for the succour of the poor in opposition to the prevailing theories of *laisser-faire*; and to assert the essential role of the great personality, the 'hero', in defiance of the tendency of the time to sink men in 'movements'.

¶ JOCELIN OF BRAKELOND
From PAST AND PRESENT

JOCELIN, we said, was somewhat of a Boswell; but unfortunately, by Nature, he is none of the largest, and distance has now dwarfed him to an extreme degree. His light is most feeble, intermittent, and requires the intensest kindest inspection; otherwise it will disclose mere vacant haze. It must be owned, the good Jocelin, spite of his beautiful childlike character, is but an altogether imperfect 'mirror' of these old-world things!...

These clear eyes of neighbour Jocelin looked on the bodily presence of King John; the very John *Sansterre*, or Lackland, who signed *Magna Charta* afterwards in Runnymead. Lackland, with a great retinue, boarded once, for the matter of a fortnight, in St. Edmundsbury Convent; daily in the very eyesight, palpable to the very fingers of our Jocelin: O Jocelin, what did he say, what did he do; how looked he, lived he—at the very lowest, what coat or breeches had he on? Jocelin is obstinately silent. Jocelin marks down what interests *him*; entirely deaf to *us*. With Jocelin's eyes we discern almost nothing of John Lackland. . . .

Jocelin notes only, with a slight sub-acidity of manner, that the King's Majesty, *Dominus Rex*, did leave, as gift for our St. Edmund Shrine, a handsome enough silk cloak,—or rather pretended to leave, for one of his retinue borrowed it of us, and *we* never got sight of it again; and, on the whole, that the *Dominus Rex*, at departing, gave us 'thirteen *sterlingii*,' one shilling and one penny, to say a mass for him; and so departed,—like a shabby Lackland as he was! 'Thirteen pence sterling,' this was what the Convent got from Lackland, for all the victuals he and his had made away with. We of course said our mass for him, having covenanted to do it,—but let impartial posterity judge with what degree of fervour!

And in this manner vanishes King Lackland; traverses swiftly our strange intermittent magic-mirror, jingling the shabby thirteen pence merely; and rides with his hawks into Egyptian night again.

Thomas Babington Macaulay

THOMAS BABINGTON MACAULAY (1800–59), afterwards Lord Macaulay, was the son of Zachary Macaulay, the man of letters and humanitarian, who played a leading part in the campaign against Slavery.

After a brilliant record at Trinity College, the younger Macaulay was called to the Bar, but made literature his chief means of support. His essay on Milton in *The Edinburgh Review* captivated Jeffrey, the Editor, and for twenty years he was one of the famous journal's outstanding contributors.

At the age of 30 he entered Parliament and made a reputation as an orator. In 1834 he became legal adviser to the Supreme

Council in India at £10,000 a year. And in 1848 he published the first two volumes of his *History of England from the Accession of James II*, which immediately caused a sensation and made him, with the possible exception of Gibbon, the most popular historian who ever wrote in English.

¶ THE SIEGE OF LONDONDERRY
From THE HISTORY OF ENGLAND FROM THE ACCESSION OF JAMES II

AT length the little squadron came to the place of peril. Then the Mountjoy took the lead, and went right at the boom. The huge barricade cracked and gave way: but the shock was such that the Mountjoy rebounded, and stuck in the mud.

A yell of triumph rose from the banks: the Irish rushed to their boats, and were preparing to board, but the Dartmouth poured on them a well-directed broadside, which threw them into disorder. Just then the Phœnix dashed at the breach which the Mountjoy had made, and was in a moment within the fence.

Meantime the tide was rising fast. The Mountjoy began to move, and soon passed safe through the broken stakes and floating spars. But her brave master was no more. A shot from one of the batteries had struck him; and he died by the most enviable of all deaths, in sight of the city which was his birthplace, which was his home, and which had just been saved by his courage and self-devotion from the most frightful form of destruction.

The night had closed in before the conflict at the boom began: but the flash of the guns was seen, and the noise heard, by the lean and ghastly multitude which covered the walls of the city. When the Mountjoy grounded, and when the shout of triumph rose from the Irish on both sides of the river, the hearts of the besieged died within them. One who endured the unutterable anguish of that moment has told us that they looked fearfully livid in each other's eyes. . . .

There was little sleep on either side of the wall. The bonfires shone bright along the whole circuit of the ramparts. The Irish guns continued to roar all night; and all night the bells of the rescued city made answer to the Irish guns with a peal of joyous defiance. Through the three following days the batteries of the enemy continued to play. But, on the third night, flames were seen arising from the camp; and, when the first of August dawned, a line of smoking ruins marked the site lately occupied by the huts of the besiegers; and the citizens saw far off the long column of pikes and standards retreating up the left bank of the Foyle towards Strabane.

So ended this great siege, the most memorable in the annals of the British Isles. It had lasted a hundred and five days.

John Henry Newman

JOHN HENRY NEWMAN (1801–90), after a brilliant record at Trinity College, Oxford, took orders, and in 1833 began the publication of the *Tracts for the Times* which were a witness to the beginning of the Tractarian or Oxford Movement. As a result of a sermon on the 39 Articles he resigned in 1842 from the Church of England and in 1845 he was received into the Roman Church. In 1879 he was made Cardinal.

As a writer Newman is distinguished for the beauty and clarity of his severely plain style, of which the following (from *The Idea of a University*) is typical.

¶ DEFINITION OF A GENTLEMAN
From THE IDEA OF A UNIVERSITY

HENCE it is, that it is almost a definition of a gentleman, to say he is one who never inflicts pain. This description is both refined and, as far as it goes, accurate.

He is mainly occupied in merely removing the obstacles which hinder the free and unembarrassed action of those about him; and he concurs with their movements rather than takes the initiative himself. His benefits may be considered as parallel to what are called comforts or conveniences in arrangements of a personal nature; like an easy chair or a good fire, which do their part in dispelling cold and fatigue, though nature provides both means of rest and animal heat without them.

The true gentleman in like manner carefully avoids whatever may cause a jar or a jolt in the minds of those with whom he is cast;—all clashing of opinion, or collision of feeling, all restraint, or suspicion, or gloom, or resentment; his great concern being to make every one at their ease and at home. He has his eyes on all his company; he is tender towards the bashful, gentle towards the distant, and merciful towards the absurd; he can recollect to whom he is speaking; he guards against unseasonable allusions, or topics which may irritate; he is seldom prominent in conversation, and never wearisome. He makes light of favours while he does them, and seems to be receiving when he is conferring.

He never speaks of himself except when compelled, never defends himself by a mere retort, he has no ears for slander or gossip, is scrupulous in imputing motives to those who interfere with him, and interprets everything for the best. He is never mean or little in his disputes, never takes unfair advantage, never mistakes personalities or sharp sayings for arguments, or insinuates evil which he dare not say out. From a longsighted prudence, he observes the maxim of the ancient sage, that we should ever conduct ourselves towards our enemy as if he were one day to be our friend.

He has too much good sense to be affronted at insults, he is too well employed to remember injuries, and too indolent to bear malice. He is patient, forbearing, and resigned, on philosophical principles; he submits to pain, because it is inevitable, to bereavement, because it is irreparable, and to death, because it is his destiny.

If he engages in controversy of any kind, his disciplined intellect preserves him from the blundering discourtesy of better, though less educated minds; who, like blunt weapons, tear and hack instead of cutting clean, who mistake the point in argument, waste their strength on trifles, misconceive their adversary, and leave the question more involved than they find it. He may be right or wrong in his opinion, but he is too clear-headed to be unjust; he is as simple as he is forcible, and as brief as he is decisive.

Abraham Lincoln

ABRAHAM LINCOLN (1809–65), the son of a humble pioneer of the Middle West, rose, mainly by his remarkable powers of oratory, to the position of President of the United States. In that capacity he had to meet the menace of the secession of the Southern States, and to carry the Civil War, in the face of the pessimism of his Cabinet, to a successful conclusion. Shortly after his election for a second term of office he was murdered by a madman in a theatre in Washington.

¶ GETTYSBURG

From DEDICATORY ADDRESS AT GETTYSBURG CEMETERY, NOV. 19, 1863

FOUR score and seven years ago our fathers brought forth upon this continent a new nation, conceived in liberty, and dedicated to the proposition that all men are created equal. Now we are engaged in a great civil war, testing whether that nation, or any nation so conceived and so dedicated, can long endure. We are met on a great battle-field of that war. We have come to dedicate a portion of that field as a final resting-place of those people who here gave their lives that that nation might live. But in a larger sense we cannot dedicate, we cannot consecrate, we cannot hallow this ground. The brave men, living and dead, who struggled here, have consecrated it far above our power to add or detract. The world will little note nor long remember what we say here, but it can never forget what they did here. It is for us, the living, rather to be dedicated here to the unfinished work that they have thus far so nobly carried on. It is rather for us to be here dedicated to the great task remaining before us,—that from these honoured dead we take increased devotion to the cause for which they here gave the last full measure of devotion,—that we here highly resolve that the dead shall not have died in vain, that the nation shall, under God, have a new birth of freedom, and that the government of the people, by the people, and for the people, shall not perish from the earth.

Edward FitzGerald

BORN in 1809, FitzGerald was educated at a school in Bury St. Edmunds and Trinity College, Cambridge. He made friends with Thackeray, and later with Tennyson and Carlyle; went to France for a short while; returned to his native Suffolk; and except for a week or so now and then never again left it. Essentially a man of letters and a recluse, he was quite content to spend his whole life among his books and flowers.

He translated Calderon and wrote a Platonic dialogue entitled *Euphranor*; and he wrote some of the best letters in the language.

But it was his learning of Persian in 1853 that set him on the road to fame. For he came on the poems of Omar Khayyam and produced that translation, if translation it can be called, which has charmed millions.

¶ THE BOAT RACE
From EUPHRANOR

SHORTLY after this the rest of us agreed it was time to be gone. We walked along the fields past the church, crossed the boat-house ferry, and mingled with the crowd upon the opposite bank.

Townsmen and gownsmen, with the laced fellow-commoner sprinkled among them here and there—reading men and sporting men—Fellows, and even masters of colleges, not indifferent to the prowess of their respective crews—all these, conversing on all topics, from the slang in Bell's Life to the last new German Revelation, and moving in ever-changing groups down the banks, where, at the farthest visible bend of the river, was a little knot of ladies gathered upon a green knoll, faced and illuminated by the beams of the setting sun. Beyond which point was heard at length some indistinct shouting, which gradually increased, until 'They are off—they are coming!' suspended other conversation among ourselves: and suddenly the head of the first boat turned the corner and then another close upon it, and then a third; the crews pulling with all their might, but in perfect rhythm and order; and the crowd upon the bank turning round to follow along with them, cheering, 'Bravo, St. John's,' 'Go it, Trinity,' and waving hats and caps—the high crest and blowing forelock of Phidippus's mare, and he himself shouting encouragement to his crew, conspicuous over all—until, the boats reaching us, we also were caught up in the returning tide of spectators, and hurried back toward the boat-house, where we arrived just in time to see the ensign of Trinity lowered from its pride of place, and the eagle of St. John's soaring there instead.

Then, waiting a while to hear how it was the winner had won, and the loser had lost, and watching Phidippus engaged in eager conversation with his defeated brethren, I took Euphranor and Lexilogus, one under each arm (Lycion having strayed into better company elsewhere), and walked home with them across the meadow that lies between the river and the town, whither the dusky troops of gownsmen were evaporating, while twilight gathered over all, and the nightingale began to be heard among the flowering chestnuts of Jesus.

William Makepeace Thackeray

WILLIAM MAKEPEACE THACKERAY (1811–63), one of our greatest novelists, was born at Calcutta and educated at Charterhouse and Trinity College, Cambridge. He left without taking a degree, entered the Middle Temple, abandoned Law for journalism and fiction. His early work—*Catherine*, *A Shabby Genteel Story*, *The Great Hogarty Diamond*, *Barry Lyndon*, and so on—was moderately successful; but real fame came to him with the publication in 1847–8 of *Vanity Fair*. Thence onward he took his place beside Dickens as one of the greatest literary figures of his time; and his reputation was strengthened by *Pendennis*, *Esmond*, *The Newcomes*, and *The Virginians*.

¶ PULVIS ET UMBRA

From ESMOND

AS Esmond and the dean walked away from Kensington discoursing of this tragedy, and how fatal it was to the cause which they both had at heart; the streetcriers were already out with their broadsides, shouting through the town the full, true, and horrible account of the death of Lord Mohun and Duke Hamilton in a duel. A fellow had got to Kensington, and was crying it in the square there at very early morning, when Mr. Esmond happened to pass by. He drove the man from under Beatrix's very window, whereof the casement had been set open. The sun was shining though 'twas November; he had seen the market-carts rolling into London, the guard relieved at the Palace, the labourers trudging to their work in the gardens between Kensington and the City—the wandering merchants and hawkers filling the air with their cries. The world was going to its business again, although dukes lay dead and ladies mourned for them; and kings, very likely, lost their chances. So night and day pass away, and to-morrow comes, and our place knows us not. Esmond thought of the courier, now galloping on the north road to inform him, who was Earl of Arran yesterday, that he was Duke of Hamilton to-day, and of a thousand great schemes, hopes, ambitions, that were alive in the gallant heart, beating a few hours since, and now in a little dust quiescent.

John Bright

JOHN BRIGHT (1811–89) was one of the outstanding statesmen and economists of the Manchester school which believed in Free Trade and freedom of competition, and opposed factory legislation and other social reforms. He was President of the Board of Trade under Gladstone and held other posts, but withdrew from the Liberal Party in 1882 as a protest against Mr. Gladstone's policy of intervention in Egypt.

Bright was always a strong pacifist, and the most famous speech of this great orator was delivered in the House of Commons in 1855 in opposition to the Crimean War. The end of it is given below.

¶ THE ANGEL OF DEATH

From A SPEECH IN THE HOUSE OF COMMONS ON THE CRIMEAN WAR, *Feb.* 23, 1855

I APPEAL to the noble lord at the head of the Government and to this House; I am not now complaining of the war—I am not now complaining of the terms of peace, nor, indeed, of anything that has been done—but I wish to suggest to this House what, I believe, thousands, and tens of thousands, of the most educated and of the most Christian portion of the people of this country are feeling upon this subject, although, indeed, in the midst of a certain clamour in the country, they do not give public expression to their feelings. Your country is not in an advantageous state at this moment; from one end of the Kingdom to the other there is a general collapse of industry. Those members of this House not intimately acquainted with the trade and commerce of the country do not fully comprehend our position as to the diminution of employment and the lessening of wages. An increase in the cost of living is finding its way to the homes and hearts of a vast number of the labouring population. At the same time there is growing up—and, notwithstanding what some hon. members of this House may think of me, no man regrets it more than I do—a bitter and angry feeling against that class which has for a long period conducted the public affairs of this country. I like political changes when such changes are made as the result, not of passion, but of deliberation and reason. Changes so made are safe, but changes made under the influence of violent exaggeration, or of the violent passions of public meetings, are not changes usually approved by this House or advantageous to the country. I cannot but notice, in speaking to gentlemen who sit on either side of this House, or in speaking to anyone I meet between this House and any of those localities we frequent when this House is up—I cannot, I say, but notice that an uneasy feeling exists as to the news that may arrive by the very next mail from the East. I do not suppose that your troops are to be beaten in actual conflict with the foe, or that they will be driven into the sea; but I am certain that many homes in England in which there now exists a fond hope that the distant one may return— many such homes may be rendered desolate when the next mail shall arrive. The angel of death has been abroad throughout the land; you may almost hear the beating of his wings. There is no one, as when the firstborn were slain of old, to sprinkle with blood the lintel and the two sideposts of our doors, that he may spare and pass on; he takes his victims from the castle of the noble, the mansion of the wealthy, and the cottage of the poor and the lowly, and it is on behalf of all these classes that I make this solemn appeal.

Charles Dickens

CHARLES DICKENS (1812–70) told in *David Copperfield* (from which the first extract below comes) some of the experiences of his childhood. He had been in a blacking factory at twelve, though afterwards sent to school when the family fortunes grew better. He became first an attorney's clerk, then a parliamentary reporter, then a writer of sketches and stories for the papers, till in 1836 he was asked to write the story for some drawings of 'cockney sporting plates'. The result was the *Pickwick Papers*. After their appearance his popularity and his fame grew continuously. He is famous for his 'characters', such as Micawber, Pecksniff, and Mrs. Gamp. But he was also capable of exact quiet work such as appears in this extract. He, like Tennyson, was an example of the capacity of some of the Victorians for combining an enormous popularity with admirable achievement. His sentiment at times overflooded the dykes it should have flowed between. But if the deaths of his children are sometimes over-pathetic, their small and grave lives are usually as convincing as could be wished.

¶ DAVID'S LIBRARY
From DAVID COPPERFIELD

MY father had left a small collection of books in a little room up-stairs, to which I had access (for it adjoined my own) and which nobody else in our house ever troubled. From that blessed little room, Roderick Random, Peregrine Pickle, Humphrey Clinker, Tom Jones, the Vicar of Wakefield, Don Quixote, Gil Blas, and Robinson Crusoe, came out, a glorious host, to keep me company. They kept alive my fancy, and my hope of something beyond that place and time,— they, and the Arabian Nights, and the Tales of the Genii,—and did me no harm; for whatever harm was in some of them was not there for me; *I* knew nothing of it. It is astonishing to me now, how I found time, in the midst of my porings and blunderings over heavier themes, to read those books as I did. It is curious to me how I could ever have consoled myself under my small troubles (which were great troubles to me), by impersonating my favourite characters in them—as I did— and by putting Mr. and Miss Murdstone into all the bad ones—which I did too. I have been Tom Jones (a child's Tom Jones, a harmless creature) for a week together. I have sustained my own idea of Roderick Random for a month at a stretch, I verily believe. I had a greedy relish for a few volumes of Voyages and Travels—I forget what, now—that were on those shelves; and for days and days I can remember to have gone about my region of our house, armed with the centre-piece out of an old set of boot-trees—the perfect realisation of Captain Somebody, of the Royal British Navy, in danger of being beset by savages, and resolved to sell his life at a great price. The Captain never lost dignity, from having his ears boxed with the Latin Grammar. I did; but the Captain was a Captain and a hero, in despite of all the grammars of all the languages in the world, dead or alive.

This was my only and my constant comfort. When I think of it, the picture always rises in my mind, of a summer evening, the boys at play in the churchyard, and I sitting on my bed, reading as if for life. Every barn in the neighbourhood, every stone in the church, and every foot of the churchyard, had some association of its own, in my mind, connected with these books, and stood for some locality made famous in them. I have seen Tom Pipes go climbing up the church-steeple; I have watched Strap, with the knapsack on his back, stopping to rest himself upon the wicket-gate; and I *know* that Commodore Trunnion held that club with Mr. Pickle, in the parlour of our little village alehouse.

¶ MRS. GAMP ON STEAM-ENGINES
From MARTIN CHUZZLEWIT

IT was so amusing, that Tom, with Ruth upon his arm, stood looking down from the wharf, as nearly regardless as it was in the nature of flesh and blood to be, of an elderly lady behind him, who had brought a large umbrella with her, and didn't know what to do with it. This tremendous instrument had a hooked handle; and its vicinity was first made known to him by a painful pressure on the windpipe, consequent upon its having caught him round the throat. Soon after disengaging himself with perfect good humour, he had a sensation of the ferule in his back; immediately afterwards, of the hook entangling his ankles; then of the umbrella generally, wandering about his hat, and flapping at it like a great bird; and, lastly, of a poke or thrust below the ribs, which gave him such exceeding anguish, that he could not refrain from turning round to offer a mild remonstrance.

Upon his turning round, he found the owner of the umbrella struggling on tip-toe, with a countenance expressive of violent animosity, to look down upon the steam-boats; from which he inferred that she had attacked him, standing in the front row, by design, and as her natural enemy.

'What a very ill-natured person you must be!' said Tom.

The lady cried out fiercely, 'Where's the pelisse!' meaning the constabulary—and went on to say, shaking the handle of the umbrella at Tom, that but for them fellers never being in the way when they was wanted, she'd have given him in charge, she would.

'If they greased their whiskers less, and minded the duties which they're paid so heavy for, a little more,' she observed, 'no one needn't be drove mad by scrouding so!'

She had been grievously knocked about, no doubt, for her bonnet was bent into the shape of a cocked hat. Being a fat little woman, too, she was in a state of great exhaustion and intense heat. Instead of pursuing the altercation, therefore, Tom civilly inquired what boat she wanted to go on board of?

'I suppose,' returned the lady, 'as nobody but yourself can want to look at a steam package, without wanting to go a-boarding of it, can they! Booby!'

'Which one do you want to look at then?' said Tom. 'We'll make room for you if we can. Don't be so ill-tempered.'

'No blessed creetur as ever I was with in trying times,' returned the lady, somewhat softened, 'and they're a many in their numbers, ever brought it as a charge again myself that I was anythin' but mild and equal in my spirits. Never mind a-contradicting of me, if you seems to feel it does you good, ma'am, I often says, for well you know that Sairey may be trusted not to give it back again. But I will not denige that I am worrited and wexed this day, and with good reagion, Lord forbid!'

By this time, Mrs. Gamp (for it was no other than that experienced practitioner) had, with Tom's assistance, squeezed and worked herself into a small corner between Ruth and the rail; where, after breathing very hard for some little time, and performing a short series of dangerous evolutions with her umbrella, she managed to establish herself pretty comfortably.

'And which of all them smoking monsters is the Ankworks boat, I wonder. Goodness me!' cried Mrs. Gamp.

'What boat did you want?' asked Ruth.

'The Ankworks package,' Mrs. Gamp replied. 'I will not deceive you, my sweet. Why should I?'

'That is the Antwerp packet in the middle,' said Ruth.

'And I wish it was in Jonadge's belly, I do,' cried Mrs. Gamp; appearing to confound the prophet with the whale in this miraculous aspiration.

Ruth said nothing in reply; but, as Mrs. Gamp, laying her chin against the cool iron of the rail, continued to look intently at the Antwerp boat, and every now and then to give a little groan, she inquired whether any child of hers was going abroad that morning? Or perhaps her husband, she said kindly.

'Which shows,' said Mrs. Gamp, casting up her eyes, 'what a little way you've travelled into this wale of life, my dear young creetur! As a good friend of mine has frequent made remark to me, which her name, my love, is Harris, Mrs. Harris through the square and up the steps a-turnin' round by the tobacker shop, "Oh Sairey, Sairey, little do we know wot lays afore us!" "Mrs. Harris, ma'am," I says, "not much, it's true, but more than you suppoge. Our calcilations, ma'am," I says, "respectin' wot the number of a family will be, comes most times within one, and oftener than you would suppoge, exact." "Sairey," says Mrs. Harris, in a awful way, "Tell me wot is my indiwidge number." "No, Mrs. Harris," I says to her, "ex-cuge me, if you please. My own," I says, "has fallen out of three-pair backs, and had damp doorsteps settled on their lungs, and one was turned up smilin' in a bedstead, unbeknown. Therefore, ma'am," I says, "seek not to proticipate, but take 'em as they come and as they go." Mine,' said Mrs. Gamp, 'mine is all gone, my dear young chick. And as to husbands, there's a wooden leg gone likeways home to its account, which in its constancy of walkin' into wine vaults, and never comin' out again 'till fetched by force, was quite as weak as flesh, if not weaker.'

When she had delivered this oration, Mrs. Gamp leaned her chin upon the cool iron again; and looking intently at the Antwerp packet, shook her head and groaned.

'I wouldn't,' said Mrs. Gamp, 'I wouldn't be a man and have such a think upon my mind!—but nobody as owned the name of man, could do it!'

Tom and his sister glanced at each other; and Ruth, after a moment's hesitation, asked Mrs. Gamp what troubled her so much.

'My dear,' returned that lady, dropping her voice, 'you are single, ain't you?'

Ruth laughed, blushed, and said 'Yes'.

'Worse luck,' proceeded Mrs. Gamp, 'for all parties! But others is married, and in the marriage state; and there is a dear young creetur a-comin' down this mornin' to that very package, which is no more fit to trust herself to sea, than nothin' is!'

She paused here to look over the deck of the packet in question, and on the steps leading down to it, and on the gangways. Seeming to have thus assured herself that the object of her commiseration had not yet arrived, she raised her eyes gradually up to the top of the escape-pipe, and indignantly apostrophised the vessel:

'Oh, drat you!' said Mrs. Gamp, shaking her umbrella at it, 'you're a nice spluttering nisy monster for a delicate young creetur to go and be a passinger by; ain't you! *You* never do no harm in that way, do you? With your hammering, and roaring, and hissing, and lamp-iling, you brute! Them confugion steamers,' said Mrs. Gamp, shaking her umbrella again, 'has done more to throw us out of our reg'lar work and bring ewents on at times when nobody counted on 'em (especially them screeching railroad ones), than all the other frights that ever was took. I have heerd of one young man, a guard upon a railway, only three years opened—well does Mrs. Harris know him, which indeed he is her own relation by her sister's marriage with a master sawyer—as is godfather at this present time to six-and-twenty blessed little strangers, equally unexpected, and all on 'em named after the Ingeins as was the cause. Ugh!' said Mrs. Gamp, resuming her apostrophe, 'one might easy know you was a man's inwention, from your disregardlessness of the weakness of our naturs, so one might, you brute!'

John Lothrop Motley

JOHN LOTHROP MOTLEY (1814–77), one of the most famous of American historians, had a distinguished record at Harvard, Göttingen, and Berlin before passing into the Diplomatic Service. He was American Minister in Vienna from 1861 to 1867, and in London in 1869–70. He lived a long time in England and died at Frampton Court, Dorchester.

But he is not remembered as a diplomat nor as the author of several novels. His greatest work was *The Rise of the Dutch Republic*, which was published in London in 1856 and brought him immediate fame. He also wrote *A History of the United Netherlands* in 1860–68 which was another great success.

His style, of which the following estimate of William the Silent (from *The Dutch Republic*) is a fair specimen, is clear and vigorous and at times lofty and noble.

¶ WILLIAM OF ORANGE
From THE DUTCH REPUBLIC

HE possessed, too, that which to the heathen philosopher seemed the greatest good—the sound mind in the sound body. His physical frame was after death found so perfect that a long life might have been in store for him, notwithstanding all which he had endured.

The desperate illness of 1574, the frightful gunshot wound inflicted by Jaureguy in 1582, had left no traces. The physicians pronounced that his body presented an aspect of perfect health. His temperament was cheerful. At table, the pleasures of which, in moderation, were his only relaxation, he was always animated and merry, and this jocoseness was partly natural, partly intentional. In the darkest hours of his country's trial, he affected a serenity which he was far from feeling, so that his apparent gaiety at momentous epochs was even censured by dullards, who could not comprehend its philosophy, nor applaud the flippancy of William the Silent.

He went through life bearing the load of a people's sorrows upon his shoulders with a smiling face. Their name was the last word upon his lips, save the simple affirmative, with which the soldier who had been battling for the right all his lifetime commended his soul in dying 'to his great Captain, Christ'. The people were grateful and affectionate, for they trusted the character of their 'Father William', and not all the clouds which calumny could collect ever dimmed to their eyes the radiance of that lofty mind to which they were accustomed, in their darkest calamities, to look for light. As long as he lived he was the guiding-star of a brave nation, and when he died the little children cried in the streets.

James Anthony Froude

JAMES ANTHONY FROUDE (1818–94) was a patriotic historian. The term is not used disparagingly, although Froude's accuracy has been challenged, but as descriptive of that sort of history in which he produced his best effects. He was a great friend of Carlyle's, and he thought he saw working in history the same doctrines that his friend preached as moral truths. But his *History of England* remains, after Macaulay, one of the most vivid histories we have. Nothing could prevent Froude having a real sense of real people or a dramatic sense of dramatic moments.

¶ THE TAKING OF THE '*CACAFUEGO*'
From ENGLISH SEAMEN IN THE SIXTEENTH CENTURY

DRAKE began to realise that he was now entirely alone, and had only himself and his own crew to depend on. There was nothing to do but to go through with it, danger adding to the interest. Arica was the next point visited. Half a hundred blocks of silver were picked up at Arica. After Arica came Lima, the chief depot of all, where the grandest haul was looked for. At Lima, alas! they were just too late. Twelve great hulks lay anchored there. The sails were unbent, the men were ashore. They contained nothing but some chests of reals and a few bales of silk and linen. But a thirteenth, called by the gods *Our Lady of the Conception*, called by men *Cacafuego*, a name incapable of translation, had sailed a few days before for the isthmus, with the whole produce of the Lima mines for the season. Her ballast was silver, her cargo gold and emeralds and rubies. Drake deliberately cut the cables of the ships in the roads, that they might drive ashore and be unable to follow him. The *Pelican* spread her wings, every feather of them, and sped away in pursuit. He would know the *Cacafuego*, so he learnt at Lima, by the peculiar cut of her sails. The first man who caught sight of her was promised a gold chain for his reward. A sail was seen on the second day. It was not the chase, but it was worth stopping for. Eighty pounds' worth of gold was found, and a great gold crucifix, set with emeralds said to be as large as pigeons' eggs. They took the kernel. They left the shell. Still on and on. We

JAMES ANTHONY FROUDE

learn from the Spanish accounts that the Viceroy of Lima, as soon as he recovered from his astonishment, despatched ships in pursuit. They came up with the last plundered vessel, heard terrible tales of the rovers' strength, and went back for a larger force. The *Pelican* meanwhile went along upon her course for 800 miles. At length, when in the latitude of Quito and close under the shore, the *Cacafuego*'s peculiar sails were sighted, and the gold chain was claimed. There she was, freighted with the fruit of Aladdin's garden, going lazily along a few miles ahead. Care was needed in approaching her. If she guessed the *Pelican*'s character, she would run in upon the land and they would lose her. It was afternoon. The sun was still above the horizon, and Drake meant to wait till night, when the breeze would be off the shore, as in the tropics it always is.

The *Pelican* sailed two feet to the *Cacafuego*'s one. Drake filled his empty wine-skins with water and trailed them astern to stop his way. The chase supposed that she was followed by some heavy-loaded trader, and, wishing for company on a lonely voyage, she slackened sail and waited for him to come up. At length the sun went down into the ocean, the rosy light faded from off the snows of the Andes; and when both ships had become invisible from the shore, the skins were hauled in, the night wind rose, and the water began to ripple under the *Pelican*'s bows. The *Cacafuego* was swiftly overtaken, and when within a cable's length a voice hailed her to put her head into the wind. The Spanish commander, not understanding so strange an order, held on his course. A broadside brought down his mainyard, and a flight of arrows rattled on his deck. He was himself wounded. In a few minutes he was a prisoner, and *Our*

Lady of the Conception and her precious freight were in the corsair's power. The wreck was cut away; the ship was cleared; a prize crew was put on board. Both vessels turned their heads to the sea. At daybreak no land was to be seen, and the examination of the prize began. The full value was never acknowledged. The invoice, if there was one, was destroyed. The accurate figures were known only to Drake and Queen Elizabeth. A published schedule acknowledged to twenty tons of silver bullion, thirteen chests of silver coins, and a hundredweight of gold, but there were gold nuggets besides in indefinite quantity, and 'a great store' of pearls, emeralds, and diamonds. The Spanish Government proved a loss of a million and a half of ducats, excluding what belonged to private persons. The total capture was immeasurably greater.

Drake, we are told, was greatly satisfied. He thought it prudent to stay in the neighbourhood no longer than necessary. He went north with all sail set, taking his prize along with him. The master, San Juan de Anton, was removed on board the *Pelican* to have his wound attended to. He remained as Drake's guest for a week, and sent in a report of what he observed to the Spanish Government. One at least of Drake's party spoke excellent Spanish. This person took San Juan over the ship. She showed signs, San Juan said, of rough service, but was still in fine condition, with ample arms, spare rope, mattocks, carpenter's tools of all descriptions. There were eighty-five men on board all told, fifty of them men-of-war, the rest young fellows, ship-boys and the like. Drake himself was treated with great reverence; a sentinel stood always at his cabin door. He dined alone with music.

George Eliot
(*Mary Ann Evans*)

GEORGE ELIOT (MARY ANN EVANS—1819–80), novelist. Her great books—such as *Adam Bede*, *The Mill on the Floss*, *Scenes of Clerical Life*, *Romola*—have all similar characteristics; they present a high nobility of action against a tragic background and amid the concerns and humours of the common people (though her Florentine populace in *Romola* is less convincing than her English rustics). She wrote as if she had a message, and this has spoiled her books for some readers. But since that message is largely one of simple endurance and effort the didacticism is lost in the humanity.

¶ MAGGIE AND THE DOLL
From THE MILL ON THE FLOSS

'MAGGIE, Maggie,' exclaimed Mrs. Tulliver, sitting stout and helpless with the brushes on her lap, 'what is to become of you, if you're so naughty? I'll tell your aunt Glegg and your aunt Pullet when they come next week, and they'll never love you any more. O dear, O dear! look at your clean pinafore, wet from top to bottom. Folks 'ull think it's a judgment on me as I've got such a child—they'll think I've done summat wicked.'

Before this remonstrance was finished, Maggie was already out of hearing, making her way towards the great attic that ran under the old high-pitched roof, shaking the water from her black locks as she ran, like a Skye terrier escaped from his bath. This attic was Maggie's favourite retreat on a wet day, when the weather was not too cold; here she fretted out all her ill-humours, and talked aloud to the worm-eaten floors and the worm-eaten shelves, and the dark rafters festooned with cobwebs; and here she kept a Fetish which she punished for all her misfortunes. This was the trunk of a large wooden doll, which once stared with the roundest of eyes above the reddest of cheeks; but was now entirely defaced by a long career of vicarious suffering. Three nails driven into the head commemorated as many crises in Maggie's nine years of earthly struggle; that luxury of vengeance having been suggested to her by the picture of Jael destroying Sisera in the old Bible. The last nail had been driven in with a fiercer stroke than usual, for the Fetish on that occasion represented aunt Glegg. But immediately afterwards Maggie had reflected that if she drove many nails in, she would not be so well able to fancy that the head was hurt when she knocked it against the wall, nor to comfort it, and make believe to poultice it, when her fury was abated; for even aunt Glegg would be pitiable when she had been hurt very much, and thoroughly humiliated, so as to beg her niece's pardon. Since then she had driven no more nails in, but had soothed herself by alternately grinding and beating the wooden head against the rough brick of the great chimneys that made two square pillars supporting the roof. That was what she did this morning on reaching the attic, sobbing all the while with a passion that expelled every other form of consciousness—even the memory of the grievance that had caused it. As at last the sobs were getting quieter, and the grinding less fierce, a sudden beam of sunshine, falling through the wire lattice across the worm-eaten shelves, made her throw away the Fetish and run to the window. The sun was really breaking out; the sound of the mill seemed cheerful again; the granary doors were open; and there was Yap, the queer white-and-brown terrier with one ear turned back trotting about and sniffing vaguely, as if he were in search of a companion. It was irresistible. Maggie tossed her hair back and ran down-stairs, seized her bonnet without putting it on, peeped, and then dashed along the passage lest she should encounter her mother, and was quickly out in the yard, whirling round like a Pythoness, and singing as she whirled, 'Yap, Yap, Tom's coming home!' while Yap danced and barked round her, as much as to say, if there was any noise wanted he was the dog for it.

Walt Whitman

WALT WHITMAN (1819–92) has too often enjoyed a notoriety greater than his reputation, and even now is more widely named than read. Born in Long Island, New York, he was at 13 an apprentice to a printer, at 17 a travelling schoolmaster, at 19 a journalist; later on, a carpenter and builder. In 1861 the American Civil War broke out, and Whitman took part in it on the side of the North, but in the care of the wounded, on the battlefields and in the hospitals. From this experience arose some of his most famous poems. Their danger is the change of tone from 'singing' to shouting. But at its best the solemn assurance, the subdued magniloquence, of this verse has been rarely surpassed; it is aware at once of humanity as a whole and the nature of which humanity is a part, and of the infinite variations within it.

Whitman's prose is less known, but, if never so final, sometimes more attractive.

¶ STARLIGHT, AND CARLYLE DYING
From SPECIMEN DAYS IN AMERICA

FOR the last three years we in America have had transmitted glimpses of a thin-bodied, lonesome, wifeless, childless, very old man, lying on a sofa, kept out of bed by indomitable will, but, of late, never well enough to take the open air. I have noted this news from time to time in brief descriptions in the papers.

A week ago I read such an item just before I started out for my customary evening stroll between eight and nine. In the fine cold night, unusually clear (Feb. 5, '81), as I walk'd some open grounds adjacent, the condition of Carlyle, and his approaching—perhaps even then actual—death, filled me with thoughts eluding statement, and curiously blending with the scene. The planet Venus, an hour high in the west, with all her volume and lustre recover'd (she has been shorn and languid for nearly a year), including an additional sentiment I never noticed before—not merely voluptuous, Paphian, steeping, fascinating—now with calm commanding seriousness and hauteur—the Milo Venus now. Upward to the zenith, Jupiter, Saturn, and the moon past her quarter, trailing in procession, with the Pleiades following, and the constellation Taurus, and red Aldebaran. Not a cloud in heaven. Orion strode through the south-east, with his glittering belt—and a trifle below hung the sun of the night, Sirius. Every star dilated, more vitreous, nearer than usual. Not as in some clear nights when the larger stars entirely outshine the rest. Every little star or cluster just as distinctly visible, and just as nigh. Berenice's hair showing every gem, and new ones. To the north-east and north the Sickle, the Goat and kids, Cassiopeia, Castor and Pollux, and the two Dippers. While through the whole of this silent indescribable show inclosing and bathing my whole receptivity, ran the thought of Carlyle dying. (To soothe and spiritualize, and, as far as may be, solve the mysteries of death and genius, consider them under the stars at midnight.)

And now that he has gone hence, can it be that Thomas Carlyle, soon to chemically dissolve in ashes and by winds, remains an identity still? In ways perhaps eluding all the statements, lore, and speculations of ten thousand years—eluding all possible statements to mortal sense—does he yet exist, a definite, vital being, a spirit, an individual—perhaps now wafted in space among those stellar systems, which, suggestive and limitless as they are, merely edge more limitless, far more suggestive systems? I have no doubt of it. In silence, of a fine night, such questions are answer'd to the soul.

John Ruskin

JOHN RUSKIN (1819-1900), having suffered some neglect, is returning into his proper place. He began his career with *Modern Painters*, written from 1843 to 1860, in which he laid down the principles of painting and incidentally asserted the greatness of Turner. His concerns were enlarged to architecture, morals, economics, education, and all social interests until he became one of the great 'prophets' of the century. He was a master of long sentences (it will be noticed that the whole extract below consists of only five), but these have in their solemn procession a moral earnestness which is not in the complex sonorities of Sir Thomas Browne or the carefully arranged visions of De Quincey.

¶ A CATHEDRAL CLOSE
From THE STONES OF VENICE

AND now I wish that the reader, before I bring him into St. Mark's Place, would imagine himself for a little time in a quiet English cathedral town, and walk with me to the west front of its cathedral. Let us go together up the more retired street, at the end of which we can see the pinnacles of one of the towers, and then through the low grey gateway, with its battlemented top and small latticed window in the centre, into the inner private-looking road or close, where nothing goes in but the carts of the tradesmen who supply the bishop and the chapter, and where there are little shaven grass-plots, fenced in by neat rails, before old-fashioned groups of somewhat diminutively and excessively trim houses, with little oriel and bay windows jutting out here and there, and deep wooden cornices and eaves painted cream colour and white, and small porches to their doors in the shape of cockle-shells, or little, crooked, thick, indescribable wooden gables warped a little on one side; and so forward till we come to larger houses, also old-fashioned, but of red brick, and with gardens behind them, and fruit walls, which show here and there, among the nectarines, the vestiges of an old cloister arch or shaft, and looking in front on the cathedral square itself, laid out in rigid divisions of smooth grass and gravel walk, yet not uncheerful, especially on the sunny side, where the canons' children are walking with their nurserymaids. And so, taking care not to tread on the grass, we will go along the straight walk to the west front, and there stand for a time, looking up at its deep-pointed porches, and the dark places between their pillars where there were statues once, and where the fragments, here and there, of a stately figure are still left, which has in it the likeness of a king, perhaps indeed a king on earth, perhaps a saintly king long ago in heaven; and so higher and higher up to the great mouldering wall of rugged sculpture and confused arcades, shattered, and grey, and grisly with heads of dragons and mocking fiends, worn by the rain and swirling winds into yet unseemlier shape, and coloured on their stony scales by the deep russet-orange lichen, melancholy gold; and so, higher still, to the bleak towers, so far above that the eye loses itself among the bosses of their traceries, though they are rude and strong, and only sees like a drift of eddying black points, now closing, now scattering, and now settling suddenly into invisible places among the bosses and flowers, the crowd of restless birds that fill the whole square with that strange clangour of theirs, so harsh and yet so soothing, like the cries of birds on a solitary coast between the cliffs and sea.

Think for a little while of that scene, and the meaning of all its small formalisms, mixed with its serene sublimity. Estimate its secluded, continuous, drowsy felicities, and its evidence of the sense and steady performance of such kind of duties as can be regulated by the cathedral clock; and weigh the influence of those dark towers on all who have passed through the lonely square at their feet for centuries, and on all who have seen them rising far away over the wooded plain, or catching on their square masses the last rays of the sunset, when the city at their feet was indicated only by the mist at the bend of the river.

Matthew Arnold

MATTHEW ARNOLD (1822–88), though now more famous as a poet, is remembered also for his prose. The son of Thomas Arnold, the famous headmaster of Rugby, he was educated at Winchester, Rugby, and Balliol, won the Newdigate Prize for poetry in 1843, and became Fellow of Oriel in 1845. In 1851 Lord Lansdowne, whose private secretary he had been for four years, appointed him inspector of schools, and he held that post for over 30 years. From 1857 to 1867 he was, in addition, professor of poetry at Oxford.

It is in his essays—*Essays in Criticism, Culture and Anarchy, Literature and Dogma,* and so on—that he is at his best: graceful but not too mannered, scholarly without being too pedantic, satirical at times, and in the best sense 'popular'. The following is typical of his style.

¶ CHARM OF OXFORD

NO, we are all seekers still! seekers often make mistakes, and I wish mine to redound to my own discredit only, and not to touch Oxford. Beautiful city! so venerable, so lovely, so unravaged by the fierce intellectual life of our century, so serene!

'There are our young barbarians all at play!'

And yet, steeped in sentiment as she lies, spreading her gardens to the moonlight, and whispering from her towers the last enchantments of the Middle Age, who will deny that Oxford, by her ineffable charm, keeps ever calling us nearer to the true goal of all of us, to the ideal, to perfection—to beauty in a word, which is only truth seen from another side?—nearer, perhaps, than all the science of Tübingen. Adorable dreamer, whose heart has been so romantic! who hast given thyself so prodigally, given thyself to sides and to heroes not mine, only never to the Philistines! home of lost causes, and forsaken beliefs, and unpopular names, and impossible loyalties! what example could ever so inspire us to keep down the Philistine in ourselves, what teacher could ever so save us from that bondage to which we are all prone, that bondage which Goethe, in those incomparable lines on the death of Schiller, makes it his friend's highest praise (and nobly did Schiller deserve the praise) to have left miles out of sight behind him; the bondage of '*was uns alle bändigt*, DAS GEMEINE'.

She will forgive me, even if I have unwittingly drawn upon her a shot or two aimed at her unworthy son; for she is generous, and the cause in which I fight is, after all, hers. Apparitions of a day, what is our puny warfare against the Philistines, compared with the warfare which this queen of romance has been waging against them for centuries, and will wage after we are gone?

George Meredith

GEORGE MEREDITH (1828–1909) used to be thought obscure. This has happened to many great writers whose meaning has afterwards been taken easily enough. But in Meredith's case the comment is justified. He *was* obscure, and his obscurity increased with the number of his novels. 'More brain, O Lord, more brain', was his demand, and he gave the readers of his novels (such as *One of our Conquerors*) opportunity to exercise what they had. But this obscurity is lightened by many lovely lucidities, many pages of beautiful emotion or intellectual comedy. The extract given below from *The Amazing Marriage* is an example of the first of these. For Meredith had an intense appreciation of nature, and communicated it; and in nature purified by intellect he put most of his belief.

The Amazing Marriage appeared in 1895, and was the last of his novels. From then till his death he was the chief authority in literature, receiving the homage of younger writers, and accepting the Order of Merit in 1905.

❡ DAWN IN THE MOUNTAINS
From THE AMAZING MARRIAGE

BEYOND the firwood light was visibly the dawn's. Half-way down the ravines it resembled the light cast off a torrent water. It lay on the grass like a sheet of unreflecting steel and was a face without a smile above. Their childhood ran along the tracks to the forest by the light, which was neither dim nor cold, but grave; presenting tree and shrub and dwarf growth and grass austerely, not deepening or confusing them. They wound their way by borders of crag, seeing in a dell below the mouth of the idle mine begirt with weedy and shrub-hung rock, a dripping semicircle. Farther up they came on the flat juniper and crossed a wet ground-thicket of whortleberry: their feet were in the moist moss among sprigs of heath; and a great fir tree stretched his length, a peeled multitude of his dead fellows leaned and stood upright in the midst of scattered fire-stained members, and through their skeleton limbs the sheer precipice of slate-rock of the bulk across the chasm, nursery of hawk and eagle, wore a thin blue tinge, the sign of warmer light abroad.

'This way, my brother!' cried Carinthia, shuddering at a path he was about to follow.

Dawn in the mountain-land is a meeting of many friends. The pinnacle, the forest-head, the latschen-tufted mound, rock-bastion and defiant cliff and giant of the triple peak, were in view, clearly lined for a common recognition, but all were figures of solid gloom, unfeatured and bloomless. Another minute and they had flung off their mail and changed to various indented, intricate, succinct in ridge, scar and channel; and they had all a look of watchfulness that made them one company. The smell of rock-waters and roots of herb and moss grew keen; air became a wine that raised the breast high to breathe it; an uplifting coolness pervaded the heights. What wonder that the mountain-bred girl should let fly her voice. The natural carol woke an echo. She did not repeat it.

'And we will not forget our home, Chillon,' she said, touching him gently to comfort some saddened feeling.

The plumes of cloud now slowly entered into the lofty arch of dawn and melted from brown to purple-black. The upper sky swam with violet; and in a moment each stray cloud-feather was edged with rose, and then suffused. It seemed that the heights fronted East to eye the interflooding of colours, and it was imaginable that all turned to the giant whose forehead first kindled to the sun: a greeting of god and king.

On the morning of a farewell we fluctuate sharply between the very distant and the close and homely: and even in memory the fluctuation occurs, the grander scene casting us back on the modestly nestling, and that, when it has refreshed us, conjuring imagination to embrace the splendour and wonder. But the wrench of an immediate division from what we love makes the things within reach the dearest, we put out our hands for them, as violently-parted lovers do, though the soul in days to come would know a craving, and imagination flap a leaden wing, if we had not looked beyond them.

'Shall we go down?' said Carinthia, for she knew a little cascade near the house, showering on rock and fern, and longed to have it round her.

They descended, Chillon saying that they would soon have the mists rising, and must not delay to start on their journey.

The armies of the young sunrise in mountain-lands neighbouring the plains, vast shadows, were marching over woods and meads, black against the edge of golden; and great heights were cut with them, and bounding waters took the leap in a silvery radiance to gloom; the bright and dark-banded valleys were like night and morning taking hands down the sweep of their rivers. Immense was the range of vision scudding the peaks and over the illimitable Eastward plains flat to the very East and sources of the sun.

Algernon Charles Swinburne

ALGERNON CHARLES SWINBURNE (1837–1909) is a poet whose reputation is still undergoing change. His books seemed to many of the Victorians terrible and outrageous; by the end of the century they had become habitual; and at the time of his death they seemed almost dull. But, for all his loss of present favour, Swinburne will have to be judiciously re-established. His criticism demands this almost more than his verse, for his prose style often hides the justice of his critical decisions by the tumult of his verbiage. Lucidity was a gift not often allowed to Swinburne. But it was present in his verse at its best, and (more continuously and more frequently) in his appreciation of literature.

¶ BYRON
From Introduction to a SELECTION FROM THE WORKS OF LORD BYRON

HIS work was done at Missolonghi; all of his work for which the fates could spare him time. A little space was allowed him to show at least a heroic purpose, and attest a high design; then, with all things unfinished before him and behind, he fell asleep after many troubles and triumphs. Few can ever have gone wearier to the grave; none with less fear. He had done enough to earn his rest. Forgetful now and set free for ever from all faults and foes, he passed through the doorway of no ignoble death out of reach of time, out of sight of love, out of hearing of hatred, beyond the blame of England and the praise of Greece. In the full strength of spirit and of body his destiny overtook him, and made an end of all his labours. He had seen and borne and achieved more than most men on record. 'He was a great man, good at many things, and now he has attained this also, to be at rest.'

Walter Pater

WALTER PATER (1839-1894) spent the greater part of his life lecturing on Philosophy at Oxford, where he was a Fellow of Brasenose College. His mind was steeped in Plato, and Platonism colours all his works. He was the author of a number of philosophical and critical writings, of which *Renaissance Studies* and the philosophical novel, *Marius the Epicurean*, are the best known. His style is academic, but has a veiled opalescent beauty.

¶ MONA LISA
From THE RENAISSANCE

THE presence that thus rose so strangely beside the waters is expressive of what in the ways of a thousand years men had come to desire. Hers is the head upon which all 'the ends of the world are come,' and the eyelids are a little weary. It is a beauty wrought out from within upon the flesh, the deposit, little cell by cell, of strange thoughts and fantastic reveries and exquisite passions. Set it for a moment beside one of those white Greek goddesses or beautiful women of antiquity, and how would they be troubled by this beauty, into which the soul with all its maladies has passed? All the thoughts and experience of the world have etched and moulded there, in that which they have of power to refine and make expressive the outward form, the animalism of Greece, the lust of Rome, the reverie of the middle age with its spiritual ambition and imaginative loves, the return of the Pagan world, the sins of the Borgias. She is older than the rocks among which she sits; like the vampire, she has been dead many times, and learned the secrets of the grave; and has been a diver in deep seas, and keeps their fallen day about her; trafficked for strange webs with Eastern merchants: and, as Leda, was the mother of Helen of Troy, and, as

Saint Anne, the mother of Mary; and all this has been to her but as the sound of lyres and flutes, and lives only in the delicacy with which it has moulded the changing lineaments and tinged the eyelids and the hands. The fancy of a perpetual life, sweeping together ten thousand experiences, is an old one; and modern thought has conceived the idea of humanity as wrought upon by, and summing up in itself, all modes of thought and life. Certainly Lady Lisa might stand as the embodiment of the old fancy, the symbol of the modern idea.

Thomas Hardy

THOMAS HARDY (1840–1928) achieved in his life three separate reputations—as a novelist, as a lyric poet, and as the writer of that 'epic-drama' *The Dynasts*. Much of the present vogue of the novel as a means for expressing 'criticism of life' may have been due to the fact that he and Meredith, each a novelist, each with a philosophy, if not a gospel, were contemporaries. Each of them also had a profound sense both of the vast and the small in nature. But while Meredith held nature, rightly apprehended, to be helpful to man, in Hardy it tends to form a background to, and to be the cause of, man's conflict, tragedy, and despair. Since, however, he was a great artist, he was capable—as here—of presenting great natural events in their detached being. Such is the famous description of Egdon Heath in *The Return of the Native* (1878) and the extract given below.

Hardy began his career in an architect's office and by writing poetry. But he abandoned both for fiction until after *Jude the Obscure* in 1895, when he returned to verse. He accepted the Order of Merit in 1910.

¶ MIDNIGHT ON ST. THOMAS'S EVE
From FAR FROM THE MADDING CROWD

THE sky was clear—remarkably clear—and the twinkling of all the stars seemed to be but throbs of one body, timed by a common pulse. The North

Star was directly in the wind's eye, and since evening the Bear had swung round it outwardly to the east, till he was now at a right angle with the meridian. A difference of colour in the stars—oftener read of than seen in England—was really perceptible here. The sovereign brilliancy of Sirius pierced the eye with a steely glitter, the star called Capella was yellow, Aldebaran and Betelgueux shone with a fiery red.

To persons standing alone on a hill during a clear midnight such as this, the roll of the world eastward is almost a palpable movement. The sensation may be caused by the panoramic glide of the stars past earthly objects, which is perceptible in a few minutes of stillness, or by the better outlook upon space that a hill affords, or by the wind, or by the solitude; but whatever be its origin the impression of riding along is vivid and abiding. The poetry of motion is a phrase much in use, and to enjoy the epic form of that gratification it is necessary to stand on a hill at a small hour of the night, and, having first expanded with a sense of difference from the mass of civilized mankind, who are dream-wrapt and disregardful of all such proceedings at this time, long and quietly watch your stately progress through the stars. After such a nocturnal reconnoitre it is hard to get back to earth, and to believe that the consciousness of such majestic speeding is derived from a tiny human frame.

Robert Louis Stevenson

EVERY one knows—or has heard of—*Treasure Island*. But this extract shows that Robert Louis Stevenson (1850–94), its author, felt the daring spirit of *Treasure Island* at home as well as in the South Seas. R. L. S. is perhaps rather unduly in the shade now; the slight attitudizing of which readers are sometimes conscious both in his style and in his life has been put down to choice rather than to the struggle of his courage with his ill-health. In his enthusiasm his pose is lost, and not only adventures and prize-fighters but style itself were among his enthusiasms. Some of his stories are among the best that have been done—lucid, swift, sustained to their culmination.

¶ THE ENGLISH ADMIRALS
From VIRGINIBUS PUERISQUE

ALMOST everybody in our land, except humanitarians and a few persons whose youth has been depressed by exceptionally æsthetic surroundings, can understand and sympathise with an Admiral or a prize-fighter. I do not wish to bracket Benbow and Tom Cribb; but, depend upon it, they are practically bracketed for admiration in the minds of many frequenters of ale-houses. If you told them about Germanicus and the eagles, or Regulus going back to Carthage, they would very likely fall asleep; but tell them about Harry Pearce and Jem Belcher, or about Nelson and the Nile, and they put down their pipes to listen. I have by me a copy of *Boxiana*, on the fly-leaves of which a youthful member of the fancy kept a chronicle of remarkable events and an obituary of great men. Here we find piously chronicled the demise of jockeys, watermen, and pugilists—Johnny Moore, of the Liverpool Prize Ring; Tom Spring, aged fifty-six; 'Pierce Egan, senior, writer of *Boxiana* and other sporting works'—and among all these, the Duke of Wellington! If Benbow had lived in the time of this annalist, do you suppose his name would not have been added to the glorious roll? In short, we do not all feel warmly towards Wesley or Laud, we cannot all take pleasure in *Paradise Lost*; but there are certain common sentiments and touches of nature by which the whole nation is made to feel kinship. A little while ago everybody, from Hazlitt and John Wilson down to the imbecile creature who scribbled his register on the flyleaves of *Boxiana*, felt a more or less shamefaced satisfaction in the exploits of prize-fighters. And the exploits of the Admirals are popular to the same degree, and tell in all ranks of society. Their sayings and doings stir English blood like the sound of a trumpet; and if the Indian Empire, the trade of London, and all the outward and visible ensigns of our greatness should pass away, we should still leave behind us a durable monument of what we were in these sayings and doings of the English Admirals.

Lytton Strachey

MR. LYTTON STRACHEY, though he has written much graceful and distinguished prose, sprang into fame as the author of one book—his *Eminent Victorians*. This was followed by his life of Queen Victoria. In this work, scholarly but graceful, satirical but never obvious or offensive—to the living, written with an effortless distinction which is Mr. Strachey's own, he set a new fashion in biography, and the book became a best-seller in America as well as in this country. The following is Mr. Strachey's description of Queen Victoria's death.

¶ THE PASSING OF QUEEN VICTORIA
From QUEEN VICTORIA

WHEN, two days previously, the news of the approaching end had been made public, astonished grief had swept over the country. It appeared as if some monstrous reversal of the course of nature was about to take place. The vast majority of her subjects had never known a time when Queen Victoria had not been reigning over them. She had become an indissoluble part of the whole scheme of things, and that they were about to lose her appeared a scarcely possible thought. She herself, as she lay blind and silent, seemed to those who watched her to be divested of all thinking—to have glided already, unawares, into oblivion.

Yet, perhaps, in the secret chambers of consciousness, she had her thoughts, too. Perhaps her fading mind called up once more the shadows of the past to float before it, and retraced, for the last time, the vanished visions of that long history—passing back and back, through the cloud of years, to older and ever older memories—to the spring woods at Osborne, so full of primroses for Lord Beaconsfield—to Lord Palmerston's queer clothes and high demeanour, and Albert's face under the green lamp, and Albert's first stag at Balmoral, and Albert in his blue and silver uniform, and the Baron coming in through a doorway, and Lord M. dreaming at Windsor with the rooks cawing in the elm trees, and the Archbishop of Canterbury on his knees in the dawn, and the old King's turkey-cock ejaculations, and Uncle Leopold's soft voice at Claremont, and Lehzen with the globes, and her mother's feathers sweeping down towards her, and a great old repeater-watch of her father's in its tortoise-shell case, and a yellow rug, and some friendly flounces of sprigged muslin, and the trees and the grass at Kensington.